Solomon Gallant-Page

English Language Structure in Context for English Second Language Learners

LONDON * CAMBRIDGE * NEW YORK * SHARJAH

Copyright © Solomon Gallant-Page 2025

All rights reserved. No part of this publication may be reproduced, distributed, or transmitted in any form or by any means, including photocopying, recording, or other electronic or mechanical methods, without the prior written permission of the publisher, except in the case of brief quotations embodied in critical reviews and certain other non-commercial uses permitted by copyright law. For permission requests, write to the publisher.

Any person who commits any unauthorized act in relation to this publication may be liable to criminal prosecution and civil claims for damages.

Ordering Information

Quantity sales: Special discounts are available on quantity purchases by corporations, associations, and others. For details, contact the publisher at the address below.

Publisher's Cataloging-in-Publication data

Gallant-Page, Solomon

English Language Structure in Context for English Second Language Learners

ISBN 9798891557727 (Paperback)

ISBN 9798891557734 (Hardback)

Library of Congress Control Number: 2025905675

www.austinmacauley.com/us

First Published 2025

Austin Macauley Publishers LLC

40 Wall Street, 33rd Floor, Suite 3302

New York, NY 10005

USA

mail-usa@austinmacauley.com

+1 (646) 5125767

To the youths of the international community who aspire to expand their horizons beyond the borders of their respective countries.

English is the *Lingua Franca.*

I would like to extend my sincere gratitude to my colleagues who have tirelessly assisted me in preparing the manuscripts of my books – Mrs NomaGcina Dondashe and Ms Noloyiso Dumezweni. Their enthusiasm to see my work published has paid off!

To my precious friend, Mr. Cecil Nogaya, with whom I've shared the love of English Language and English Literature since our college days at Cicira College of Education of the then University of Transkei. His expression of confidence that I can make it in the world of writers has been the essential impetus.

Lastly, our English Lecturer at Cicira College of Education during the late 1980s, Mrs Knight of Britain, deserves the accolade for her outstanding teaching which left an indelible impression in my heart.

To JJ Studio of Sprigg Street, Mthatha. I owe this business special thanks for the sterling service for rendering the editable version of the manuscript of my book timeously.

Table of Content

Unit 1 Simple Present Tense	10
Unit 2 Sentences	43
Unit 3 Present Continuous Tense	63
Unit 4 Simple Past Tense	73
Unit 5 Present Perfect Tense	104
Unit 6 Parts of Speech	110
Unit 7 Present Perfect Tense	124
Unit 8 Simple Future Tense	139
Unit 9 Future Continuous Tense	150
Unit 10 Parts of Speech	170
Unit 11 Parts of Speech	178
Unit 12 Parts Of Speech	195
Unit 13 Direct and Indirect Speech	205
Unit 14 Active Voice and Passive Voice	218
Unit 15 BUILDING OF WORDS	231
Unit 16 Forming of Nouns	246
Unit 17 Forming of Adjectives	256
Unit 18 The Infinitive	265
Unit 19 Proper Use of Modal Verbs	276
Unit 20 Homophones and Homonyms	285
Unit 21 Paraphrasing	300

Addendum A	322
Addendum B	324
Addendum C	327
Addendum D	328
Addendum E	333
Addendum F	338
Addendum G	340
Addendum H	342
Addendum I	343
Addendum J	349
Addendum K	355
Index	359

Unit 1
Simple Present Tense

1. Affirmative Form

1.1. How to use this tense:

This tense is used to express:

- habitual actions, for example:
  Linda wakes up at 7.
  She wakes up at 7.
  Lizo prepares breakfast at 7.
  He prepares breakfast at 7.
  Linda and Lizo wake up at 7.
  They wake up at 7.
- universal truths, for example:
  The sun rises in the East.
  The sun sets in the West.
  God is love.

- **1.2. Adverbs of time**

This tense is indicated by the following adverbs of time:
- every………for example:

    <u>Every</u> day Linda wakes up at 7.
- often, for example:

    <u>Linda</u> <u>often</u> wakes up at 7.
- seldom, for example:

    Lizo <u>seldom</u> prepares breakfast at 7.
- usually, for example:

    Linda and Lizo <u>usually</u> wake up at 7, etc.

1.3. Structure of a Simple Present Tense Sentence

- a singular subject is followed by a singular verb to which s is added, for example:

    Linda wakes up at 7.

    She wakes up at 7.
- a plural subject is followed by a plural verb to which no s is added, for example:

    <u>Linda and Lizo</u> wake up at 7.

    They wake up at 7.

1.4. Helping Verbs and Modal Verbs That Express Simple Present Tense Actions and Events:

- is: It denotes singularity, for example:

Linda is my sister.

She is my sister.

- are: It denotes plurality.

    Linda and Lizo are learners.

- can: It denotes possibility, for example:

    Linda can prepare breakfast.

- may: It denotes probability, for example

    Lizo may prepare breakfast.

- must: It denotes obligation, for example:

    Linda and Lizo must work hard in order to progress to the next grade.

2. Practising the Correct Use of the Simple Present Tense

2.1. Speaking Activity

A learner will say what the following people do in their jobs:

Note well: verbs must end with an s

Your teacher or partner will ask:

- What do the following people do?
    - A doctor
- Your answer
    - A doctor treats sick people.
    - A shoemaker
    - A cobbler

- A greengrocer
- A fish monger
- A draper
- A haberdasher
- A hawker
- An interpreter
- A milliner
- A musician
- A nurseryman
- An organist
- A pianist
- A treasurer

2.2. Writing Activity

Respond in full sentences to the questions.

- When does your mother wake up?
- What does she do at 6?
- What do you do at 6?
- When does your father go to work?
- When do you go to school?
- What do learners do at school?
- What do they do during break time?
- Who prepares supper at your home?

- Who serves supper at your home?
- Who prepares supper at your home?
- Who serves supper at your home?
- Who is your cousin?
- How old is your cousin?
- Who are your friends?
- How old are they?

2.3. Re-write this paragraph by correcting the mistakes:

Linda and Lizo Go Shopping.

Every Saturday Linda's parent send Lizo and Linda to town. She seldom ask them to go shopping during the week. Lizo and Linda enjoys to do shopping. They gets the early bus to town. They usually visits the Trader's mall where they buys specials. Their parent are happy when they returns home safe because there is bag snatchers during the weekends in town.

2.4. Consult your Social science textbook and write the paragraph in which you describe the water cycle.

2.5. Study this timetable which shows what Linda does every day. Then write a paragraph based on this time table.

0W5:30	Wake up, make her bed, wash.
06:00	Prepare and serve breakfast.
06:30	Iron uniform and polish shoes.
07:00	Dress herself.

07:30	Go to school.
07:45	Ring bell.
08:00	Participate in lessons.
10:00	Break.
10:30	Attend school library and conduct research.
12:30	Return to the classroom
13:00	Lunch break
13:30	Resume classroom activities
14:00	Leave school and go home.

2.6. Improve Your Vocabulary

2.6.1. Find words beginning with 'con' in your dictionary which will fit each of the following meanings.

- Use each one in a sentence:

- a group of stars forming a pattern
- a policeman
- small pieces of coloured paper thrown at a wedding.
- to muddle
- a magician
- defeat in battle
- letters of the alphabet which are not vowels
- a person serving a prison sentence

2.6.2. Use your dictionary to find some words beginning with "ex" to replace the underlined words in the following sentences and rewrite the sentences.

Check to see that you have been given the <u>precise</u> change.

Gold, diamonds and fruit are <u>sold to other countries.</u>

His paintings are <u>on public display</u> at the Port Elizabeth Art Gallery.

The athletes must go through a <u>programme of bodily movements in training</u> in order to be fit.

During holidays we often go on a <u>pleasure trip</u> to the Cango Caves of Oudsthom.

For reading activity we normally read a <u>short passage</u> from Ways of Dying by Zakes Mda.

Workmen may begin <u>to dig up</u> the road to make a new subway.

The doctor <u>inspects and tests</u> Zolas's leg to find out whether no bones have been broken after the accident.

2.6.3. Find words beginning with "ad" to fit the meaning given below. Use each word in a sentence.

- floating helplessly in the sea.
- to like and respect very much.
- a grown up.
- a senior naval officer.
- sticky, like glue.
- To allow to come in.
- To move forward.
- To offer something for sale in a newspaper or on the radio.

2.6.4. Explain the meanings of the following expressions which are used to refer to people. Then use each expression in a sentence to illustrate the meaning.

- out of sorts
- apple of her eye
- making sense
- breathing fire and fury
- let off steams
- bear a grudge
- one of the family
- had a nerve
- look up to
- narrow-minded

2.6.5. What do we call each of the following?

- an unmarried man
- an unmarried lady
- a woman whose husband is dead.
- a man whose wife is dead.
- a person who leaves his own country to settle in another.
- a settler in a new country.
- a person who lives in a rented house or flat.
- the person from whom a house or a flat is rented

2.7. Reading and Reasoning Activity

- Answer the questions that follow after you have silently read this passage entitled *Tigers* by Judy Ross from Ginn Zoo Books:

They come from many parts of Asia and live in very different climates. Some live in forests where it is cold and snowy, some live in hot, steamy rain forests, and some live in tall grass thickets.

Tigers use different sounds to communicate with each other. They snarl when they are angry and sometimes hiss and lash their tails. The roar of a tiger can be heard from far away and is often the male's way of announcing that he is in his territory.

Most members of the cat family do not like water, but tigers do, and they swim very well. They need fresh water for drinking and bathing and will often stand in a stream or a river to keep cool during the heat of the day. Sometimes, when there has not been enough rain and the streams have been dried up, they have to dig holes in the stream-bed to find water.

Watching a tiger stalk its prey is a lesson in cunning and patience. Slowly it creeps forward, lifting and placing each paw gently on the ground until it is within 6 to 9 m of its prey. The tiger may then lie concealed until the animal comes close enough for it to jump.

The tiger's attack usually comes as a complete surprise.

2.7.1. How Well Did You Understand the Passage?

- Answer all questions in full sentences:
  - In which continent do we find tigers?
  - Which type of climates do tigers tolerate?

- How does a tiger show "its anger"?
- Why does a tiger sometimes roar?
- How do tigers keep themselves cool during the heat of the day?
- How do tigers get water during the drought?

2.7.2. How Many New Words Did You Learn?

- Find the word in the passage with this meaning:

   the opposite of "wild" (paragraph 3)

   clever (Paragraph 3)

   follow silently (Paragraph 3)

   an animal that is killed by another (Paragraph 3)

   moves slowly (Paragraph 3)

   hidden (Paragraph 3)

2.8. Improve Your Vocabulary

2.8.1. Whom would you associate with each of these? E.g. a farmer uses a tractor.

- compass
- church
- pulpit
- spanner
- bricks
- igloo

- palette
- joystick
- race-horse
- cell

2.8.2. Match each idiomatic expression with its right meaning chosen from below:

- to play the game
- out of sorts
- to sweep the board
- a dog in a manger
- to bury the hatchet
- a close shave
- a feather in one's cap
- to take the chair
- in the nick of time
- to turn over a new leaf.

-
  - to preside at a meeting
  - at the right moment
  - to make peace
  - to reform one's conduct
  - to win or take all
  - not feeling well

- to be very selfish
- a narrow escape
- to act fairly
- a proud achievement

2.8.3. Explain the following proverbs:

As you make your bed, so you must lie on it.

The early bird catches the worm.

Once bitten, twice shy.

New broom sweeps clean.

You cannot eat your cake and have it.

When the cat's away, the mice will play.

Every cloud has a silver lining.

What cannot be cured, must be endured.

Tell the truth, and shame the devil.

Talk of the devil, and he'll appear.

2.8. Correct Order and Paragraph Writing

Make the drawing of the water cycle before you write a paragraph describing the water cycle. Do not forget to write first the topic before you draw and describe the water cycle. The first and last sentences have been written for you.

First sentence:

Water falls from the clouds as rain and reaches the earth.

Last sentence:

Then the clouds became cooler and cause rain to fall, and so the whole cycle begins again.

3. Simple Present Tense: Negative Form

3.1. Structure of a sentence

- s + does not+ stem of verb e.g. Tom does not go……
- s + do not + stem of the verb e.g. Tom and Mary do not go……

Therefore, the negative form of singular verbs and plural verbs respectively is:

- goes > does not go
- writes > does not write
- speaks > does not speak
- go > do not go
- write > do not write
- speak > do not speak, etc.

* In the case of helping verbs and modal verbs we put "not" after a helping verb or modal verb to make a sentence NEGATIVE, e.g.

- am > am not
- is > is not
- are > are not

- will > will not
- shall > shall not
- may > may not
- can > cannot
- must > must not

3.2. Make the following negative:

- He breaks a cup.
- They break a cup.
- She likes oranges.
- I like oranges.
- She comes early.
- We come early.
- A bird flies high.
- Birds fly high.
- He teaches Maths.
- They teach Maths.
- The thief runs away.
- Thieves run away.
- He is my brother.
- They are my brothers.
- He can break a brick.
- You may come.
- They must go now.

- He will like this activity.
- We shall come late.
- She has two oranges.

3.3. Simulation Activity

As a prefect you have been asked to write classroom rules on a poster in which you state what the students must NOT do.

The heading of the poster must be CLASSROOM RULES and the rules must be numbered consecutively. The first rule has been written for you:

Do not make noise.

3.4. Study this table which shows what Bongani does every day.

1. gets up	06:00 am
2. eats breakfast	07:30 am
3. buys lunch	13:00 pm
4. reads a newspaper	13:20 pm
5. listens to music	17:30 pm
6. visits a friend	17:50 pm
7. goes for a walk	18:00 pm
8. watches television	18:30 pm
9. enjoys supper	19:30 pm
10. sleeps	21:00 pm

- Now answer in full sentences the questions that are based on this table:
- Does Bongani get up at 7:00 am?

- When does he get up?
- Does Bongani eat breakfast at 6:00 am?
- When does he eat breakfast?
- Does Bongani buy lunch at 12:00 pm?
- When does he buy lunch?
- Does Bongani read a newspaper at 13:00 pm?
- When does he read a newspaper?
- Does Bongani listen to music at 17:00 pm?
- When does he listen to music?
- Does Bongani visit a friend?
- When does he visit a friend?
- Does Bongani go for a walk at 18:30 pm?
- When does he go for a walk?
- Does Bongani watch television?
- When does he watch television?
- Does Bongani enjoy supper at 19:00 pm?
- When does he enjoy supper?
- Does Bongani sleep at 20:00 pm?
- When does he sleep?

3.5. Improve Your Vocabulary

3.5.1. Draw this crossword puzzle and use your dictionary to help you solve the clues. Some of the letters have been provided.

1 P	A 2	3	4			5	▓	6
7 A				▓		8		N
9			1	10 N	11 G		▓	
12		D					▓	
		D		13			14 L	
	▓		15			N		
16	17 R			▓				▓
18		T		19		▓		▓
	▓	20			▓	21 E		

CLUES ACROSS

1	Boil for a short time.
7	A region or the measurement of a surface.
8	A long period of time, apparently without end.
9	News.
12	They are in charge of Newspaper.
13	Implements.
15	A girl's name.
16	Part of the circumference of a circle.
18	A small quantity.
20	A note added to the end of a letter (abbreviation).
21	To be.

CLUES DOWN

1	Fatherly.
2	Very dry, waterless.
3	Re-addresses a letter.
4	Food used to entice fish.
5	Something to learn.
6	A conjunction meaning "except when" or "if not".
10	Famous.
11	A sailor's drink.
14	A mixture of rum and water.
17	Vegetables belonging to the onion family.
19	To tear.

3.5.2. Use the words below in sentences which illustrate their meanings clearly:

technical technician technology technologist technological

machine mechanically mechanism

invent inventor invention inventive

electric electricity electrical electronic electrician

industry industrial industrialist industrialisation industrious

3.5.3. Write sentences to explain what each of the following person do for a living:

a stewardess

a matron

a cashier

a receptionist

a short-hand typist

a civil engineer

an estate agent

a journalist

a hardware salesman

3.5.4. Use one of the words from the list below in place of the underlined words in the following sentence:

Busy, grouse, vegetarian, competitor, genius, annually, sculptor, hermit, boy, sculpture, biennially

In a cave in the mountains lives a <u>man who lives entirely by himself</u>.

Juno always finds something to <u>grumble and complain</u> about.

The motor race is held <u>once a year</u> in Kyalami.

We usually have salad and fruit when my cousin comes to lunch because he is a <u>person who eats</u> no meat.

As well as being a famous painter, Helen Sebidi is also a <u>carver of statues</u>.

Nelson Mandela is a <u>person of great gifts and intelligence</u>.

A <u>floating marker</u> is usually placed near the wreck to warn other ships to keep clear.

The spiked shoes belong to a <u>someone taking part</u> in the Marathon.

3.5.5. Match each word in the list below with its partner and then use each pair of words in a sentence to illustrate its meaning:

Sound, tongs, low, starts, go, tom, parcel, sweet, means, ready.

Part and…

Ways and…

Touch and…

Harmer and…

Fits and…

Rough and…

High and…

Short and…

Safe and…

Tattered and…

3.5.6. Make up sentences to show the differences in meanings between the following pairs of words.

lend, borrow

who's, whose

taught, learned

accept, except

beat, won

there, their

lay, laid

3.5.7. Rewrite the following sentences replacing the underlined word with one chosen from the list below:

Amusing, embarrassed, dismal, gaudy, minute, indignant, famished, exhausted.

When Pinda opened her watch, one of the <u>small</u> screws fell out on the floor.

After their long journey through the bush, the hunters were <u>tired</u>.

That was a <u>very funny</u> story which Thoko told.

Fay was wearing a <u>very colourful</u> dress yesterday.

The children were feeling <u>hungry</u> as usual.

Joe was <u>much too shy</u> to go to the stage to make the speech.

Mr Koekermoer was <u>angry</u> when he saw the neighbour's car parked in front of his driveway.

Tuesday was a <u>dull</u> day, and we did not go out.

3.5.8. Draw the shapes of the following:

A meandering river

A corrugated roof

A domed roof

A spiral staircase

An oval ball

A wedge of cake

A hairpin bend

A crescent moon

3.5.9. Match each of the meanings in the left-hand column with the correct word in the right-hand column. Use each word in a sentence.

Column A	Column B
a) A woman who gives a party	Traitor
b) One who is unable to pay his debts	Invalid
c) A person who offers his services	Volunteer
d) A man who betray his country	Hostess
e) A person who is sick or disabled	Bankrupt

3.6. Articles

- Types of Articles

3.6.1. The Indefinite Article:

- a
- an

The indefinite article refers to a single, unspecific thing and is followed by a singular noun.

"A" is used when the word following it begins with a consonant sound:

- A student always studies books.

"An" is used before a word that begins with a vowel sound:

- An honest student does not cheat.

Note well:

Some vowels which have the same sound as consonants must be preceded by "a"

- A useless tool
- A university
- A eulogy
- A one-sided point of view

3.6.2. The Definite Article

- The definite article refers to a specific, particular thing or specific, particular things.
- The sun sets in the West.
- The winter months are not hot.

A. Write the following sentences in plural:

A dog is vicious.

A potato is rich in fibre.

A student is always good.

A chair is made of wood.

A man is brave.

An eye is blue or brown.

A cow gives milk.

An airport is a busy place.

A garden has a tree.

An apple grows on a tree.

B. Write the following in singular:

Horses are animals.

Balls are toys.

Novels are books.

Watches are small clocks.

Tables are pieces of furniture.

Roses are beautiful flowers.

Frenchmen are Europeans.

Children are not always good.

There are always tables in dining rooms.

Exercises are not always easy for beginners.

4. Simple Present Tense: Question Form

4.1. Question by simple inversion

* It is used when the verb form contains an auxiliary verb in which case the subject is placed immediately after that verb, and a question mark is placed at the end of the sentence:

- He can read English. (statement)
- Can he read English? (question)
- He is a student. (statement)
- Is he a student? (question)

- When the verb form does not contain an auxiliary verb, use is made of the verb "does" or "do" to formulate a question:
- Joe likes tea. (statement)
- Does Joe like tea? (question)
- They like tea. (statement)
- Do they like tea? (question)

4.1.1. Make the following statements questions:

She has a brother.

He must do it now.

She is very late.

They have time to do it.

You can wait here.

I am right.

We can see from here.

He must eat it.

They are Afrikaaners.

She can put it on the table.

He sells nice biscuits.

You speak good Afrikaans.

It smells good.

I write well.

He takes French lessons.

They often go to the cinema.

They play basketball.

He lives in the neighbourhood.

She feels uneasy.

He loves his children.

He drives to work.

I do it right.

He believes she is innocent.

It costs R50.00.

We keep them inside the yard.

She swims well.

We write to them every week.

They have two cars.

He has a car.

She does her homework.

4.1.2. Read this passage carefully

Lizo is my elder brother. He is 16 years this year. He helps me when I do my homework. I enjoy working with him because he is always friendly.

* Form at least 5 questions that are based on this preceding passage.

4.1.3. Write suitable questions to which these would be the answers:

No, she can't drive properly.

Yes, I like tea.

It leaves at 7:00 am.

My father has a garage.

We attend morning classes.

4.2. Improve Your Vocabulary

4.2.1. Use the following doubles to complete the sentences below:
- Spick and span
- Lock and key
- High and low
- Over and over
- Sick and tired
- Rough and ready
- Hammer and tong
- Neck and neck
- Cut and dry
- Pick and choose

My wife keeps our bedroom……

Warders keep convicts under……

She always searches………for her bedroom keys.

Visitors do not………as they please in these premises.

My mother tells us………that we must work very hard at school.

Although this house is well-built, but it looks very……

That parent and the principal often go for each………during the SGB meetings.

I cannot do otherwise the deal is……

There comes the horses, they run……! Which one is the winner?

She always dresses smart because she………her clothes from

4.2.2. Use the following idiomatic expressions in sentences that show you understand the meanings of these idiomatic expressions:

to be taken aback.

To be on the alert.

The apple of one's eye.

To turn one's back upon.

With open arms.

Bad blood.

a bag of bones.

to bear in mind.

to bite the dust.

to look back.

4.2.3. Explain the following proverbs:

Give a dog a bad name and hang him.

What the eyes do not see, the heart does.

Easier said than done.

Fine feathers make fine birds.

Forewarned is forearmed.

God helps those who help themselves.

Many hands make light work.

You may lead a horse to water, but you cannot make it drink.

People who live in glass houses should not throw stones.

Strike the iron while it is hot.

4.3. Spelling

- o Rule: words containing ei and ie.
- o "I" comes before "a" except after c, and when the ei represents the sound ay:

  believe, relief, siege (i before e) receive, deceit, ceiling (ei follows c) neighbour, weight, eight (ei sounds ay).

- The following are some words which do not follow this rule:

  Leisure, weird, seize, neither, sheik, weir, height.

- After the sh sound, the combination is used, even when sh is represented by c:

  ancient, efficient, species.

4.3.1. Use the above rule to identify words spelt incorrectly. Correct the words.

4.3.2. Thief, chief, receipt, neice, shield, piece, brief.

4.3.3. Reign, veil, niegh, friend, sieze, freight, vien.

4.3.4. Decieve, relieve, yield, quotient.

4.4. Reading and Reasoning You and Your Financial Future

Forecasts are that we will have a higher economic growth this year. This is positive for jobs and businesses opportunities in the light of the declining inflation and interest rates.

These are the most important features of our economy. These positive forecasts can only be spoiled by upward pressure on inflation and interest rates due to higher imports, declining balance of payments, pressure on our reserves, pressure on our Rand, exchange rate and growing demand for credit.

This should be counteracted by: the Reserve bank's determination to protect the Rand against inflation and rapid exchange rate falls, and a likely inflow of foreign money both in investments and loans.

In short the implications are:

- Inflation will probably decline slowly by a percentage point or two,
- Interest rates will probably be a percentage point or two lower by the year end.

These conditions have always favoured two investment categories:

Property and Shares

Section A: Learn About New Words

- Fill in the missing words:
  - Forecasts in this passage are good because they predict the………..of our

economy.

- In this passage positive is to as………negative is to bad.
- The opposite of declining is………
- Inflation is the general………in prices which negatively affects the………of money.
- Internal rate is the applicable amount of money you are charged for using the………of another.
- Balance of payments is the………in value between payments into and out of a country.
- People buy on………if they are sold goods or services which they shall pay in full later.
- The Rand exchange rate relates to the………of our Rand in relation to the currencies.

Section B: Understanding the Passage

Answer all questions in full sentences. You are encouraged to use your own words.

- What happens when a country experiences economic growth?
- Briefly explain why the declining inflation and interest rates are regarded as the most important features of our economy.
- Mention 5 factors that have the negative influence on inflation and interest rates.
- Who is the governor of the South African Reserve Bank?
- What is the function of the Reserve bank?
- Explain what you understand about shares and property regarded as the best

forms of investments?
- Where can an investor buy shares in South Africa?

Unit 2
Sentences

5. What Is a Sentence?

An English sentence follows an SVO pattern, i.e. subject, verb and object. It expresses a complete thought. It always begins with a capital letter and ends with a.

- Full stop.
- Question mark.
    Or
- Exclamation mark.

A sentence may be expressed in three forms:

a statement, e.g.:
   He lives in Queenstown.
a question, e.g.:
   Does he live in Queenstown?
a command, e.g.:
   Go to Queenstown.
Or a request, e.g.:

Please go to Queenstown.

Or a prohibition, e.g.:

Do not go to Queenstown.

Or an exclamation, e.g.:

What a beautiful town!

5.1. Practising Activity

Say which of the following are sentences and which are not, and if they are sentences, say which of them are:

(statements (ii) questions (iii) commands (iv) requests (v) prohibitions (vi) exclamations

- Insert the necessary punctuation marks.

Do you live in Queenstown

What an exciting journey

It is my favourite subject

If the sun shines brightly

Please reply me

How angry he is

Do help him if you can

Gathering her belongings and walking out of the house.

Do not talk to him

Give him three of them.

5.2. Subject and Predicate

A complete sentence makes sense only if it contains two essential parts:

- A naming part called the subject.
- A doing part or telling part called the predicate.

For example:

SUBJECT	PREDICATE
Lizo	Prepares breakfast at 7
His sister	Washes the plates

NOTE WELL:

- The subject is found by asking "who" or "what" before the verb, e.g.:

    Who prepares breakfast at 7? Lizo (subject)

    Who washes the plates? His sister (subject)

- The predicate contains the verb and the object of a sentence. Always find the verb first. In order to find out whether a verb has an object, it is necessary to add the question words "whom", "what" and "which" to the verb e.g.:

    Prepares what? "breakfast" is the object of "prepares"

    Washes what? "the plates" is the object of "washes"

Therefore, we can divide a sentence as follows:

Subject	Predicate	
	Verb	Object
Lizo	Prepares	Breakfast at 7.
His sister	Washes	The plates.

5.3.1. Practising Activity

Divide each sentence into its subjects and predicate.

Langa wakes up at 6.

He makes his bed.

His sister prepares breakfast.

He polishes his school shoes and her sisters.

Their father drives them to school.

5.3.2. Divide each of the above sentences into:

(a) the subject (b) the verb (c) the object.

5.3.3. REMEMBER: A singular subject takes a singular verb e.g. <u>Lizo prepares breakfast</u>. A singular verb has s.

A plural subject takes a plural verb, e.g. <u>Lizo and Lizie prepare</u> breakfast. A plural verb does not have s.

Add a suitable subject to each of the following:

………emits carbon monoxide.

………hibernate in winter.

………commit crime.

………grow in the desert.

………preaches the gospel.

………makes furniture.

………passes laws of the land.

………fixes leaky taps.

………keeps food fresh.

5.3.4. Re-arrange the words in such a way that a sentence is formed from each of the strings of words under the topic: MISTAKES WINNERS DON'T MAKE.

art part time teaches a neighbour of mine.

about complains she being always broke.

fundamental she doesn't truth understand.

financial capital accrue or to human capital either all rewards in life.

financial capital over nobody has control.

5.4. Parts of Speech

A sentence consists of parts of speech which have specific function towards the sense of a sentence. Parts of speech are simply words that constitute a sentence when arranged accordingly.

- Noun

  It is a word that names:

  A place, e.g. Pretoria

  A person, e.g. Kawuta Kosani

  A month, e.g. April

  A day of a week, e.g. Sunday

  A thing, e.g. book

  An idea, e.g. happiness

5.4.1. Classification of Nouns

- **PROPER NOUNS**

  They are names of persons, places, rivers, month and days of the week.

COMMON NOUNS

  They are names of common things

- **ABSTRACT NOUNS**

  Nouns that name qualities in persons, creatures or things e.g. beauty, kindness, happiness etc.

- **COLLECTIVE NOUN**

  It is the name of a group or a collection of people or things, e.g. a bunch of keys etc.

REMEMBER:

In a sentence, a noun may either serve as the SUBJECT or OBJECT of a sentence.

5.4.2. Practising Activity

Complete the following paragraph by filling in the suitable nouns:

A serious………always studies before he sleeps. ……..like hardworking………because stand a good chance to become successful……… when they finish their………. likewise, watchful………are also part and parcel of the excellent……….of their children. Therefore,………must work hand in hand with parents.

SUITABLE NOUNS TO CHOOSE FROM:

Parents, Student, Teachers, Students, Adults, Studies, Performance

Use the following pairs of nouns in full correct sentences:

builder, bricks

carpenter, cupboards

greengrocer, vegetables

tobacconist, tobacco

cashier, bank

cabinet maker, furniture

auctioneer, highest bidder

hosier, stockings

ironmonger, hardware

milliner, women's hats

nurseryman, plants and trees

outfitter, clothes

plumber, taps and pipes

usherette, seat

upholsterer, chairs and car seats

Fill in the names of these receptacles (containers) by choosing from the list below:

A......of perfume

A......of cutlery

A......of pickles

A......of sweets

A......of cigarettes

A ......of flowers

A......of oranges

A......of paraffin

A......of bananas

A......of peaches

A......of tea

A......of meal

A......of oil

A......of fruit

A......of jewels

bowl, basket, pocket, box, canteen, box, drum, tin, crate, bag, tray, carton, flask, bottle, jar.

5.4.3. The Plural Form of Nouns

For spelling purpose, let us consider the following rules that govern the formation of plural forms:

Where the singular form of the noun ends in s, ss, ch, sh, x, the plural is formed by adding -es.

Where the singular form of the noun ends in y, and y is preceded by a vowel, add an s, e.g. boy – boys.

If there is a consonant before the y, change the y to i and add es, e.g. story – stories.

Where the singular form of the noun ends in o, add either s or an es to form the plural:

- Tomato – tomatoes
- Photo – photos

Nouns that end in f or fe <u>sometimes</u> change the f to v before adding s or es to form the plural.

Irregular plurals are formed from the following singular nouns. You must memorize this category of singular nouns and their corresponding plural form:

Singular	Plural
Man	Men
Woman	Women
Child	Children
Tooth	Teeth
Goose	Geese
Foot	Feet
Mouse	Mice
Ox	Oxen
Index	Indices/indexes
Appendix	Appendices/appendixes
Analysis	Analyses
Basis	Bases
Oasis	Oases
Parenthis	Parentheses

Nouns whose singular form is the same for the plural form:

- Salmon
- Trout
- Deer
- Gross
- Heathen
- Sheep
- Cannon

Note well: Memorise this category.

Nouns that have no singular form :
- Mathematics
- Statistics
- Billiards
- Scissors
- Tongs
- Trousers

5.4.4. Practising Activity

REMEMBER:

- Only countable nouns take "a" or "an".
- Uncountable nouns do not take "a" or "an", and usually have no plural.

Put the following in plural

An empty bus travels fast.

A bare tree does not sway.

A high shelf is safe for a child.

A good photo changes hands like a good painting.

A loud cry often shocks people.

A steep cliff is dangerous.

A brave hero does not fear death.

An old piano takes space unnecessarily.

A red ruby sparkles in the dark.

A green valley makes a good pasture for cattle.

A steel buoy can hold a ship.

A fresh loaf smells nice.

A tall chimney emits smoke to the neighbourhood.

A wife is a woman.

A potato is a vegetable.

Put the following in singular:

Plump babies are healthy.

High roofs are easily flown away by strong winds.

Ripe tomatoes have nice aroma.

Dwarfs are mythical creatures

Red cherries decorate wedding cakes.

Strong men do perfect labour intensive jobs.

Big oxen pull ploughs and heavy wagons with ease.

Free libraries belong to municipalities.

Clever thieves do not escape the police net.

Silk scarves remain scarce and expensive.

Cool oases save lives in deserts.

My scissors are blunt.

Lively trout drift southwards in summer.

Healthy sheep graze in the veld.

Good books have clear indices.

5.5. Types of Sentences

Basically, there are three types of sentences

Simple Sentence

- It has a finite verb (a full, complete verb as compared to a non-finite verb such as a gerund or participle) e.g.:

The dog is barking.

Compound Sentence

- It consists of two complete sentences that are joined together with a conjunction e.g.

    The dog is barking and chasing the thief, (joining two sentences)
- conjunctions

    And, but, or
- "and" means in addition.
- "but" means on the contrary and is used to contrast one idea with another.
- "or" helps to point out an alternative.

Complex Sentence

- It consists of one main clause and one or more subordinate clauses (adjectival, adverbial, noun) e.g.

    The dog is barking and chasing the thief that is running away.

CLAUSE

- It is a group of words containing a finite verb and is dependent on another group of words containing a finite verb.

- The dependant group is called a subordinate clause (noun, adjectival, adverbial). It depends for its sense on the main clause.
- The main clause often can stand alone e.g.

Main clause: The dog is barking and chasing the thief.

Subordinate clause: that is running away.

5.5.1. Enlarging a Simple Sentence

- It can be made bigger adjectivally, e.g.

    The <u>vicious black</u> dog is barking <u>during the night</u>.

5.5.2. Practising Activity

Use the following verbs to build logical (correctly ordered) Simple sentences:

NB: Use a proper noun once.

wakes up

opens

makes

sweeps

washes

prepares

serves

irons

polishes

goes

Use the following verbs to build logical compound sentences with the help of the conjunctions: and, but, or:

NB: Use the proper nouns once.

wake up

open

make

sweep

wash

prepare

serve

iron

polish

go

Enlarge the following simple sentences adjectivally and adverbially.

Remember: An adjectival enlargement always tells the reader about a <u>noun</u> i.e. what he/she/it/they look like. On the other hand, an adverbial enlargement always tells the reader about a <u>verb</u> i.e. how/why/when the action takes place.

A businessman serves customers.

An advertisement increases profit.

Sales drop.

House prices go up.

Oil price affects standard of living.

5.5.3. The Writing of Complex Sentences with The Aid of Relative Pronouns (Who, which, that, whom, whose)

- Adjectival Clause as Subordinate Clause:

    This type of clause begins with a relative pronoun that describes the noun in the MAIN CLAUSE:

    This is the lesson. I like the lesson, (that)

    This is the lesson that I like.

    "that I like" describes "the lesson".

REMEMBER:

- WHO, WHOM, WHOSE, and THAT refer to persons,
- WHICH and THAT refer to things.

"THAT" is less formal. "WHO" and "WHICH" are more formal.

Join the Two Sentences with Who, Which, That, Whose, Whom

　　This is the greengrocer. The greengrocer is our neighbour.

　　We buy fresh vegetables from the greengrocer.

　　The greengrocer is our neighbour.

This is Peter. His father is the greengrocer.

Customers like Peter. They also buy vegetables from Peter.

Students deserve to repeat grades. Students fail to study properly.

The activities must be done. The teacher gives us activities.

Lizo intends to be the chartered accountant. He is intelligent and hardworking.

Where is the homework? I asked you to submit the homework today.

Can you remember the rules of using the relative pronouns correctly? You have just read the rules.

She is a diligent student. We expect the brilliant future of her.

Complete each sentence by adding a definition beginning with WHO or WHICH or THAT:

A surgeon is a………e.g. a surgeon is a doctor who operates on patients.

A locksmith is a……….

A barber is a……….

A chef is a……….

A hawker is a……….

A disc-jockey is a……….

A carburettor is a……….

A legume is a……….

A conifer is a……….

A periscope is a……….

A recipe is a……….

An advertisement is a……….

A tenant is a……….

A lease is an……….

A landlord is a………….

5.6. Reading and Reasoning Activity

- Answer the questions that follow after you have silently read this passage entitled *Grow your own vegetables.*

Vegetables contain many important minerals and vitamins that keep our bodies healthy. With food prices going up all the time, it makes a lot of sense to start growing your own vegetables. Best of all it's easy, it costs very little, and you'll probably have a lot of fun doing it!

If you don't have a garden of your own, get together with community members and see if you can identify a piece of local land that can be used for a community garden. Or find out whether somebody else in the neighbourhood has a piece of land that you can use in a way that benefits you both.

Steps of Growing Vegetables:

In a sunny part of your garden, dig a trench about two meters long, one metre wide and half a metre deep. Keep the topsoil separate from the deeper soil.

Collect as much organic waste as you can find, including raw vegetables and fruit peels or scraps, raw egg shells, newspaper, cardboard, teabags, wood ash, raw bones and mealie cobs. Pour it all into the bottom of the trench, wet it thoroughly and then cover it, first with deeper soil, then top soil.

Rake the surface even and make shallow grooves across the width of the bed about 20 cm apart and 1 cm deep for small seeds, and about 30 cm apart and 2.5 cm deep for longer ones like cabbages, peas and bush beans. Now plant the seeds carefully in the grooves, cover them with soil and water gently (read the seed packets for further instructions).

Water your seeds regularly for the first ten days and after those two to three times a week, keeping the soil slightly moist.

5.6.1. How Well Did You Understand the Passage?

Answer all questions in full sentences:

    State three reasons why it is good for people to grow their own vegetables.

    Why must a vegetable garden be in a sunny part?

    Of what importance is the organic waste to the growing of vegetables?

    Explain how the seeds of cabbages are planted.

    Why should the seed bed be kept moist?

How Many New Words Did You Learn?

- Find the word in the passage that means:

significant (paragraph 1)

the opposite of healthy (paragraph 1)

to locate/find (paragraph 2)

opposite of top (paragraph 4)

thrice (paragraph 6)

Understand Your Grammar

    Give the singular of the five common nouns in paragraph 1.

    Form abstract nouns from the following words:

- Healthy
- Growing
- Own
- See
- Identity
- Deep
- Wide
- Separate

Choose five abstract nouns that you have formed above and use them in compound sentences and complex sentences.

Analyse the following complex sentence into MAIN CLAUSE and SUBORDINATE CLAUSE

- Vegetables contain many important minerals and vitamins that keep our bodies healthy.

With food prices going up all times, it makes a lot of sense to start growing your own vegetables

Unit 3
Present Continuous Tense

6. Affirmative Form.

6.1. How to Use This Tense

This tense is used to express:

an action that is taking place at the moment of which we are speaking now.
a future action.

6.2. Adverbs of Time

This tense is indicated by the following adverbs of time:

o   At the moment, e.g.

    He/she/it is feeling pain at the moment because of the accident.

    They/we/you are feeling bad about the news at the moment.

    I am feeling uneasy at the moment.

- **NOW**

  He/she/it is feeling pain now.

  They/we/you are feeling bad now.

  I am feeling uneasy now.

- **TOMORROW**

  He/she is leaving for Durban tomorrow.

  They/we/you are returning on Friday.

  I am returning home in two weeks' time.

6.3. Structure of the Simple Present Continuous Tense

- Singular subject + auxiliary is + present participle form of a verb e.g. He/she/it is playing.

- Plural subject + auxiliary are + present participle form of a verb, e.g. They/we/you are playing.

- Singular + auxiliary am + present participle form of a verb, e.g.

I am playing.

6.4. Practising the Correct Use of the Present Continuous Tense

6.4.1. Speaking Activity

The teacher will order the learners to perform the following actions respectively and ask a student, as well as the class to respond verbally:

Teacher	Stand up P
	(P will stand up)
Teacher	What are you doing, P?
Student	....
Teacher	Class, what is she doing?
Class	....
Teacher	P and Q stand up
	(P and Q will stand up)
	What are you doing?
Students	....
Teacher	Class, what are they doing?

Here are further instructions to practise the present continuous tense:

Read from a book, write on the board, fetch a piece of chalk, bring me a pencil, go into the comer, and cut some paper.

Remember the Difference Between the Simple Present and Present Continuous Tenses:

- Simple present tense expresses habitual actions and general truths.
- Present continuous tense tells us about an action that is happening NOW AT THIS MOMENT

6.4.2. Writing Activity

- Supply a suitable simple present tense or present continuous tense of the given verb:
  - She (go) to school every day,
  - We now (learn) English.
  - The sun always (shine) in Egypt.
  - I (sit) on a chair and eat a banana.
  - Bad students never (work) hard.
  - It (rain) in winter. It (rain) now.
  - I (wake up) at 7 and (Have) breakfast at 7:30
  - He generally (sing) in English but today he (sing) in French.
  - The teacher (point) at the chalkboard when he (want) to explain something.
  - Mother (cook) some food in the kitchen at present. She always (cook) in the mornings.
  - The sun (rise) in the east, now it (set) and nightfall.
  - That man in the white hat who walk past the window (live) next door.
  - Architect (make) plans of buildings.
  - I wear a coat because the sun (not shine).
  - I always (meet) you on the corner of this street.
  - The baby (cry) because it is hungry now.

- I (spend) this weekend in Westbourne. I (go) there nearly every week.
- "Where are you?" "I (sit) in the kitchen." "What you (do) there?" "I (help) my mother."
- "Why you (wash) these clothes this morning?" "Because the sun (shine). I never (wash) clothes when there are clouds in the sky."
- "Where you (go) now?" "I (go) to the theatre." "I (go) tonight also, but I (not go) very often." "I (go) every week, but tonight I (go) for the second time in three days."

NOTE WELL:

The following verbs are never used in the PRESENT CONTINUOUS TENSE. These are mainly verbs of condition or behaviour not strictly under human control, as a result they go on whether we like it or not:

- See
- Have
- (posses/own)
- Hear
- Notice
- Recognise
- Smell (when intransitive)
- Taste (when intransitive)
- Believe
- Feel
- Think
- Know

- Understand
- Remember
- Recollect
- Forget
- Suppose
- Mean
- Gather
- Want
- Wish
- Forgive
- Refuse
- Love
- Hate
- (dis) like
- Care
- Sen
- Appear (=seem)
- Belong to
- Consist of
- Matter

Exceptional uses of these verbs are more frequent in spoken English, in particular the present continuous with always or for ever, meaning "at all times" e.g.

- You're always seeing something stronger.
- My sister is for ever refusing to wash dishes.

7. Present Continuous Tense: Negative Form

7.1. Structure of a Sentence

- Singular subject + auxiliary is + not + present participle form of the verb e.g.

He/she/it is not playing.

- Plural subject + auxiliary are + not present participle form of the verb, e.g.
- They/we/you are not playing.

Singular subject + auxiliary am + not + present participle form of the verb, e.g.
I am not playing.

8. Improve Your Vocabulary

8.1. Study the share guide of the business section of a local newspaper and explain what the following abbreviations stand for and entail:

JSE > Johannesburg Securities Exchange. This is where shares of listed companies are bought and sold by investors.

S

DM

YM %

DY

PE

DV

8.2. Name the place where

- Fire engines are housed.
- Wild animals are protected in their natural state.
- Motor cars are repaired.
- grain is stored
- Women's hair is set
- Aero planes are housed.
- Plants are grown out of season.
- Experiments in chemistry are carried out.
- Clothes are washed and ironed
- Books are kept.
- Money is coined.
- Dead bodies are kept before burial.
- Stuffed animals and antiques can be seen.
- Young plants are grown
- Fruit is grown.
- Doctors perform operations.
- Water and trees are found in the desert.
- Orphans are housed.
- Medicines are sold.
- Electricity is generated

8.3. Show in sentences that each of these words has two different meanings

- Bear
- Stamp
- Down
- Race
- Dart
- Mine
- Plot
- Bar
- Bit
- Saw
- Well
- Watch
- Round
- Shoot
- Fold
- Board

8.4. Replace the definition with a word beginning with q.

- A duck's cry.
- To tremble with fear.
- A fourth part

- Odd or funny
- At rest, calm
- To leave off
- A long feather
- A case for arrows
- 24 sheets of paper
- An angry dispute
- A ship's landing place.
- Answer of division sum

Unit 4
Simple Past Tense

9.1. Affirmative Form

9.1.1. How to Use This Tense

This tense is used to express the time when the event or action took place, e.g. He closed the shop at 5 pm.

- **NOTE WELL:**

The majority of English verbs form the simple past tense by adding "ed" to the stem of the verbs. These are called regular verbs e.g. closed, opened, walked etc.

Some verbs change the vowel sound within the stem to form the simple past tense, e.g.

Swim	Swam
See	Saw
Break	Broke
Come	Came

Verbs that already end in "d" or "t" make no change to form the simple past tense, e.g.

Spread	Spread
Shut	Shut
Cut	Cut
Put	Put

9.2. Adverbs of Time

This tense is indicated by the following adverbs of time:

- Yesterday e.g.

    Yesterday he studied very hard.

- Last e.g.

    Last week/month/year he studied hard.

- Ago e.g.

    Two weeks/months/years ago he studied hard.

9.3. Auxiliary verbs and modal verbs that express the simple past tense:

Is	Was
Are	Were
Has	Had
Have	Had
Will	Would
Shall	Should
May	Might
Must	Had to
Can	Could

9.4. Practising the Correct Use of the Simple Past Tense

9.4.1. Speaking Activity

- Answer the following questions verbally:

    When did you last see me?

    When did you write your last homework?

    When did this lesson begin?

    What did you drink for breakfast today?

    How much did your pen cost?

    Where did you buy it?

    When did you last write with it?

    Did you go to the seaside last summer?

    How long did you spend there?

    How many cups of tea did you drink yesterday?

    Did you come here on a bicycle or by taxi?

    When did you last take an examination?

    When did you last write a letter?

    When did you last see snow?

    When did you last hear some music?

    When did you last go to the cinema? What did you see there?

    What did you take home to read last week?

    On what day last week did you visit your friend?

    When did you ride a bicycle last month?

    Where did you spend your holiday last year?

9.4.2. Put the following in Simple Past Tense

(1) I break a cup.

(2) It begins to rain.

(3) We like oranges.

(4) You cut your finger.

(5) She comes early.

(6) Birds fly high.

(7) I lie on the bed.

(8) He teaches English.

(9) The river flows to the sea.

(10) I know his name.

(11) You lie to me.

(12) The prisoner runs away

(13) He tears his coat.

(14) They have a car.

(15) We wake up at seven.

(16) Your dog bites me.

(17) It costs a lot of money.

(18) You hide the key.

(19) The river freezes in winter.

(20) They drink tea in the morning.

(21) I choose a book.

(22) The servant sweeps the room.

(23) He does his work well.

(24) That pudding smells nice.

(25) You find your bag.

(26) You wear a lovely dress.

(27) I say no.

(28) Someone steals the money.

(29) We ring the bell.

(30) You ride a bicycle.

(31) The boy throws a ball.

(32) The girl catches it.

(33) I put the book on the table.

(34) Mother makes a cup of tea.

(35) She takes a plate from the cupboard.

(36) You spend too much money.

(37) She tells us a story.

(38) I try to be useful.

(39) The red light means stop.

(40) The little boy falls down.

(41) They build a house.

(42) The sick man gets better.

(43) I eat my lunch quickly.

(44) Flowers grow in my garden.

(45) The soldier fights the enemy.

(46) I want coffee for breakfast

(47) We buy meat.

(48) He feeds his horse.

(49) She loses her way.
(50) A baker sells bread.
(51) I bend my arm.
(52) We swim in the sea.
(53) She understands everything.
(54) I see a beautiful tie in the shop window.
(55) The window blows strongly.
(56) He thinks hard.
(57) I feel it.
(58) We go out at night
(59) The picture hangs on the wall.
(60) Her knees hurts her.
(61) I use my car sparingly.
(62) We keep our handkerchiefs in the drawer.
(63) They meet outside the cinema
(64) He pays the bill timeously.
(65) I play football at school.
(66) I read a book before I go to bed.
(67) He smokes a pipe after supper.
(68) He shuts the door softly.
(69) The artist draws a picture.
(70) I write letters in the evening.
(71) She lights fire in the morning.
(72) You hear a noise.
(73) The little boy stands on a chair.

(74)   She sits down when she is tired.

(75)   We let the cat out at night.

9.4.2. Practising Activity

Re-write the short history of MaNtatisi by giving the correct form of the verbs in brackets.

The husband of MaNtatisi, Mokotjo, died in 1813, and their son, Sekonyela, was too young to become chief, so his mother (to become) chief of Batlokwa tribe.

During the reign of MaNtatisi, there (to be) Wars of Difaqane. MaNtatisi (to distinguish) herself as the great fighter who (to lead) her followers in battles in which she (to emerge) victorious. She (to be) greatly (to fear) by her enemies.

Many tribes (to want) to defeat her, but they (to fail). She (to spread) death and fear among the scattered tribes when she (to move) across the Orange River. At last MaNtatisi and her people (to come) to live at a place called Yoaloboholo. This (to be) a mountain near the Caledon River.

10. Simple Past Tense: Negative Form

10.1. Structure of a Sentence

- S + did not + stem of a verb e.g.

  Jack did not cry.

- Therefore, the negative form of "cried" is "did not cry".

- In the case of auxiliary verbs and modal verbs we put "not" after an auxiliary verb or modal verb to make a sentence NEGATIVE, e.g.

Was	Was not
Were	Were not
Would	Would not
Should	Should not
Might	Might not
Could	Could not
Had to	Had not to

10.2. Make the Following Negative

(1)   Jack went to a shop.

(2)   He bought some egg.

(3)   He paid for them.

(4)   He put them in the bag.

(5)   He lost the bag.

(6)   He left it in a bus.

(7)   Somebody found it.

(8)   Jack's mother sent him to bed.

(9)   Mr Bona rang the bell.

(10)   Sisi opened the door.

(11)   He took his hat off.

(12)   He sat down and waited.

(13)   He looked at the pictures on the wall.

(14)   He tried to read a newspaper.

(15)   The young woman came back.

(16)   She led him into another room.

(17)   Mr Phiko said good morning to him.

(18)   He sat down in an armchair.

(19) Mr Phiko stood near him.
(20) Mr Bona opened his mouth and shut his eyes.
(21) Mr Phiko frowned.
(22) Mr Bona felt uneasy.
(23) A sparrow made a nest in this tree.
(24) It laid five eggs.
(25) Duma saw the nest.
(26) He climbed the tree.
(27) He held on to a branch with one hand.
(28) He took two of the eggs.
(29) He put them in his mouth.
(30) He needed both his hands.
(31) He began to climb down.
(32) One of the branches broke.
(33) Duma fell and hurt his arm.
(34) The eggs broke too!
(35) They tasted nice.
(36) Mr Bleu knew French.
(37) He became a teacher.
(38) He taught the boys French.
(39) They showed him some games.
(40) Everybody laughed.

11. Past Continuous Tense: Affirmative Form

11.1. How to Use This Tense

The past continuous tense is used when we are not interested in the completion of one or more actions, but simply in the fact that they both are in progress at the time something else happens:

- When I went out the sun was shining.

It tells us one of two actions in progress at the same time:

- He was singing while I was reading the novel.

    It is also used to show repeated actions in the past:

- He was always complaining about things that could not annoy any person.

11.2. Practising Activity

- Supply suitable past tenses of the verbs in brackets:

    He (sit) in a restaurant when I (see) him.

    The boy (fall down) while he (run).

    When the match (begin) we (approach) the stadium.

    The light (go out) while we (have) supper.

    I (have) tea when the light (go out).

    My friends (sing) when I (come) into the room.

    While you (play) music I (write) a letter.

    He (eat) his breakfast when I (arrive) at his place.

    He (die) while he finish) the Comrades Marathon.

When the phone (ring), I (have) a bath.

I speak to her several times, but she always (read) and (not listen) to me.

He (close) his watch while he (see) the sights of the city.

Professor Kaschula (teach) IsiXhosa for years in UNITRA when he (live) in Mthatha and (work) as a lecturer and researcher.

I (open) the door just as Themba (knock).

The house (burn fast, so we break the window to get out.

Maisie (cook) fish when I first ask her to marry me.

We (walk) to the bridge when it (begin) to drizzle.

My little daughter (break) two cups while she (serve) tea to our guests.

When teacher (come) in, the boys (play).

She (lean) against the door and (listen) to the radio when I first (try) to speak to her.

While he (write) a letter the telephone (ring), as he (go) to answer it, he (hear) a knock at the door, the telephone still (ring) while he (walk) to the door, but just as he (open) it, it (stop).

11.3. Practising Correct Use of the Past Continuous Tense

Show the relationship between simple past tense and past continuous tense by supplying suitable form of the verbs in brackets to complete this continuous narration:

We (near) Knysna when I (look) through the window. As soon as our train (come) to a standstill, many hawkers (rush) from the seaside. We could see that they bring) bunches of various fruit, smoked fish and other delicacies. While I (leave) the train I (notice) that the rest of the passengers (argue) about the prices. I (walk) about for a few minutes and (admire) the happy street life of Knysna, people (buy) jewellery articles and painters (paint) imaginary landscapes or (carve) political figures of world acclaim!

I (return) to my train as the sun (set), the market on the train still (continue. A young artist who (sit) on the seat behind me (offer) a beautiful portrait for R500. I (talk) hard for ten minutes, and just as the ship (go) I (buy) it for R300. As I (go) to my seat I (se) a tourist with a portrait like mine. I (ask) him the price. "R200," he said, "but I (pay) a fortune for it. A man that I (talk) to just now only (pay) R50."

As I (impact) the painting, I (notice) that there (be) no signature of the painter anywhere on it!

12. Complex Sentences: Adverbial Clause

Types of Adverbial Clauses with Their Conjunctions:

12.1. PURPOSE: In order that, so that, in case, "to" when the subject of the subordinate clause is the same as that of the main clause.

- In a subordinate clause "may" follows a present tense, present perfect tense or future in the main clause and "might" follow past tense.

Examples of adverbial clauses of purpose:

He studied hard so that he may pass.

    He studied hard so that he might pass.

She studies hard in order that she might succeed.

They often take books in case they want to study.

12.2. CAUSE – as, because, since

They worked hard as/because/since they wanted to pass the examinations.

12.3. TIME – after, as, as long as, as soon as, before, by the time, directly, immediately, since, the moment, until, when, while.

- **NOTE WELL:**

Do not use future tense in the time clause.

Example of adverbial clauses of time:

He will return home after the conference is over, (not will be over).

She went out as he came in.

She stayed there as long as she could.

He left as soon as he got the results.

He left before they sent the results.

By the time the results came, he was in Cape Town on holiday.

Directly/Immediately they told him, he left.

She has worked since she arrived.

The moment he saw her he smiled.

Until he married her, he had been reclusive.

He went out when she entered.

He was talking while she was writing.

12.4. CONCESSION – although, even though, however, no matter what.

Examples of adverbial clauses of concession

They studied hard although they were time.

They were determined to go no matter what their father said.

They missed classes again even though they were warned not to yesterday.

- **NOTE WELL:**

Subordinate adverbial clauses can appear before or after the main clause. Always use a comma after an adverbial clause is placed before the main clause e.g.

He will come although he is tired.

Although he is tired, he will come.

12.5.1. Complete the Following by Using Suitable Adverbial Clause of Purpose:

- They came to the university……………
- They took extra lessons…………………
- She woke early………………………..
- He did not go too early…………………
- ……………. she left the front door open.

12.5.2. As Above with Clauses of Cause

- ………………she would not speak to them.
- His exam results were bad……………..

- ....you are going to get a prize.
- Handmade bags are expensive.....................
- She is usually late for class..........................

12.5.3. As above with clauses of TIME

He rushed out of the house...............

...............his face lit up.

I hope we meet...............

................they went to several of the new shows.

................it does not necessarily mean she is angry with him.

12.5.4. As above with clauses of CONCESSION

- ....He Is No Fool.
- They insisted on continuing................
- They were ordered to head for the border.
- ....however late you arrive.
- They were determined to master sentence writing ....

13. Improve Your Vocabulary

13.1. Use these doubles to complete the sentences below:

Odds and ends, fits and starts, thick and thin, safe and sound, ups and downs, back and call.

- Everybody has his…………….his life.
- I have an old briefcase in which I keep…………….
- Lindi wrote to say that she had arrived…………….
- Our old car goes by……………..and is reliable.
- Mrs Jill seems to be at her daughter's…………………..
- When I was in trouble, Bob stood by me through……………..

13.2. Explain the difference by means of a sentence between:

- To gorge and gorge.
- A burrow and a barrow.
- Vein, vane and vain.
- Desert and dessert.
- Stationery and stationary

13.3. Write down the meanings of these proverbs, the meanings of which are given but not in the same order:

- Look before you leap.
- Beggars cannot be choosers.
- New brooms sweep dean.
- A soft answer turneth away wrath.

- Out of sight, out of mind.
- Waste not, want not.
- A bird in the hands is worth two in the bush.
- Let sleeping dogs lie.
- A gentle remark is the best answer to any angry outburst.
- Do not stir up trouble unnecessarily.
- Something that is certain or known is better than something that is uncertain and unknown.
- If you never waste anything, you are never likely to want for anything.
- Those who have nothing are compelled to take what is offered.
- Newcomers like to introduce changes.
- When anyone is absent, he is forgotten.
- Examine the position carefully before you take action.

14. Correct Use of:

- SOME and ANY
- MUCH and MANY
- LITTLE and FEW
- EACH OTHER and ONE ANOTHER

14.1. SOME and ANY

"Some" is used in positive statements. In questions, "some" usually implies that the questioner knows the answer or that he expects an affirmative answer.

Positive Statements:

- I need some pencils
- He is ordering some refreshments.

QUESTIONS:

- Would you like some tea?
- Didn't I give you some money yesterday? I feel sure I did.

"Any" is used in negative statements. In questions, "any" usually implies that the questioner does not know the answer or that he expects a negative answer.

Negative Statements:

- I cannot find any salt.
- You did not bring any potatoes.

QUESTIONS:

- Can you find any salt?
- Did you get any pocket money yesterday?

Never mind. I will today, OK?

- **NOTE WELL:**

The same rules apply to compound words formed from "some" and "any" such as:

- Someone
- Somebody
- Something
- Anyone
- Anybody
- Anything

14.1.1. Fill in some or any as required:

- There isn't……polish in this tin.
- "Please give me………more pudding". "I'm sorry but there isn't………"
- You have………….fine flowers in your garden.
- Go and ask him for more………….paper. I haven't………in my desk.
- I have more letters for you to write.
- I like those roses, please give me. What a pity there aren't red ones.
- I can't eat……………more potatoes, but I should like more beans.
- I don't think there is…………. one here who can speak Xhosa.
- Will you have…………more tea?
- Won't you have………….more cake?
- Did you go……….where last night?

- You're expecting …………one to call, aren't you?
- Haven't I given you……….money yesterday? I feel certain I did.
- Can you give me………….more information?
- I you haven't………….money, you can get from the bank.
- Why don't you ask the bank for………….money?
- Can you get………….more money from the bank?
- You look as if you were expecting……one. Is……….friend of yours coming?
- Are you expecting…….one else? If not, we'll go…….where for a drink.
- I haven't…….time to do……more now, you can do……yourself.
- Have you…….cigarettes? Would you give me……….for my case, if you have?
- What is the use of practicing……….more rules of English grammar?
- Did you have…….trouble with your car today? I heard you had ………. yesterday.
- These aren't my books. Did I take……….of yours by mistake?
- Wouldn't you like……….thing to drink? Have……….cherry brandy?
- Have you read……….good books lately?
- Are there lemons………….in the cupboard?
- I want to buy……….flowers, we haven't……….in the garden now.

14.2. MUCH and MANY

"Much" is used with uncountable nouns which occur usually in the singular. "Many" is used only with plural nouns.

14.2.1. Add in "much" or "many" as required

- He hasn't got………money.
- You haven't done………….
- She hasn't given me……….
- There's not………coffee in this pot.
- He hasn't got………work to do.
- I haven't invited…………people to my party.
- You haven't had………to eat.
- The cook hasn't put salt in the stew.
- My brother doesn't read………books.
- She has not………children.
- You did not make………tea.
- There was not………dirt in the classroom.
- I have not heard………about it.
- Did you have………trouble?
- Did you see………people there?
- Do you smoke………cigarettes?
- We haven't had……….luck of late.
- Have you………time to spare?
- Our………problems are causing us……….trouble.
- He has had………….opportunity but he has never taken advantage of them.

14.3. LITTLE and FEW

"Little" is the opposite of "much", and "a few" is the opposite of "many". Therefore "little" is used with singular nouns and "a few" is used with plural nouns.

14.3.1. Complete these sentences by filling in: much, many, little, a few:

- We were able to stay for only………minutes.
- After last Saturday's heavy defeat, I think there will be…….changes in the Bafana Bafana.
- During the 1995 African Cup……….changes were made in the Bafana Bafana because the national team played with zeal.
- He will never learn so long as he pays so………attention
- They did not score……….points during the match.
- Do not attach………importance to it.
- The stadium stands in a prominent position. You should have…………difficulty in finding it.
- Do not rely on him. He has very………knowledge of the South African football.
- He has made………effort to improve the performance of the team, although he has been given………opportunities.

14.4. Each Other and One Another

"Each other" refers to two persons and "one another" refers to more than two persons.

14.4.1. Add in "each other" and "one another" as required:

- The two students help............
- I like student who help...............
- The teacher and students co-operate with.........to get the best results.
- Although the school and the community must interact with............... through the school governing body, the constructive criticism during the interaction must prevail over destructive criticism.
- Children, especially during break time may hurt..........if there is no code of conduct to control their actions.
- Do you often visit.............during the weekends to discuss homework's and assignments?

15. Reading and Reasoning

Read this extract from *Seven Inventors* by Harry McNicol before you answer questions that are based on it.

December 17, 1903 was a cold, windy day. On the sands at Kittyhawk, a small group of men stood, five being spectators, and other two, Orville and Wilbur Wright. In the sand was set a long, metal-covered, wooden rail, eight inches high. At one end of this rested the "Flier", very similar in shape to the Wrights's first glider, but bigger, and fitted with motor-engine, connected to two propellers behind the wings. The time was 10:30 in the morning.

All was ready and the two brothers looked at each other inquiringly. Orville produced a coin and spun it. Wilbur called wrong, and, with a grin, the other climbed into the machine, placing himself flat on the lower plane. The engine was started and, while the spectators watched breathlessly and Wilbur ran alongside, the "Flier" began to move along the rail. It gathered speed, and after traveling forty feet along the rail, rose gradually into the air to the height of eight or ten feet. For twelve seconds the machine travelled at the speed of ten miles an hour and then landed on the sand.

Three more flights were made that morning, getting longer as the brothers became more skilful with the controls. The fourth lasted nearly a minute and covered 852 feet.

You can imagine the joy of the brothers. They had been the first men to fly – as distinct from gliding in a "heavier-than-air machine". Satisfied that their machine would fly, they returned home and, during the winter, made a bigger and better one. When it was completed, they invited the newspaper men to come and see it fly, but the machine refused to behave itself that day, and the reporters went away without very much faith in the Wright brothers.

People were accustomed to hearing of men trying in vain to fly, to take much notice of the claims of the two inventors. One day a newspaper reporter lay hidden behind a hedge, watching the two brothers. When the aero plane roar into the air and flew about, he was astonished and dashed off to the post office to send the story to his paper. But the editor would not believe it and the reporter got into trouble for sending such nonsense.

How Well Did You Understand the Passage?

Answer all questions in full sentences.

- What happened on the 17 December 1903 at Kittyhawk?
- In which country is Kittyhawk?
- How many men were present to watch that spectacle?
- Quote the words that indicate the experiment took place at the sea-shoe.
- Why did the two brothers spin a coin?
- What was the purpose of the rail?
- How many flights were made that morning?
- Why was the second occasion a failure?
-   Suggest a suitable tittle to the passage?

HOW MANY NEW WORDS DID YOU LEARN?

- Find the word that means onlookers (Paragraph 1)
- The two brother _____ when they looked at each other inquiringly. (Paragraph 2)
- Forty feet is equivalent to _____ metres.
- State the difference between flying and gliding. (Paragraph 4)
- The newspaper men are _____ (Paragraph 5)
- What astonished the reporter about the aeroplane? (Paragraph 5)
- Ten miles equivalent to _____ kilometres. (Paragraph 2)

UNDERSTAND YOUR GRAMMAR

- Write the singular of 5 common nouns in paragraph 1.
- Identify 5 proper nouns in paragraph 1.
- State the simple present tense of any 5 verbs in paragraph 2.
- What type of sentence is:
- The fourth lasted nearly a minute and covered 852 feet
- When it was completed they invited the newspaper men to come and see it fly.
- Analyse the first sentence in (iv) above into:

| SUBJECT | VERB | OBJECT |

(Identify the main clause and the subordinate clause in (iv) above. State the type of the subordinate clause.

SIMPLE PAST TENSE: QUESTION FORM

16.1.1 Question by simple inversion.

*It is used when the verb form contains an auxiliary verb, in which case the subject is placed immediately after the auxiliary verb and a question mark is placed at the end of the sentence:

(e.g)

- He could speak English. (statement)
- Could he speak English? (question)
- He was a student. (statement)
- Was he a student? (question)

* When the verb form does not contain an auxiliary verb, use is made of the verb "did" to formulate a question:

- Joe liked tea. (statement)
- Did Joe like tea? (question)
- Joe broke the key. (statement)
- Did Joe break the key? (question)

- **NOTE WELL:**

The subject is placed immediately after "Did" and the stem of the verb is used. Therefore, it is wrong to say:

- Did Joe liked tea?
- Did Joe broke the key?

16.1.1. Make the Following Statements Questions:

- Jack went to a shop.

- He bought some eggs.
- He paid for them.
- He put them into a bag.
- He lost the bag.
- He left it in a bus.
- Somebody found it.
- Jack's mother sent him to bed.
- Mr Roy rang the bell.
- A young woman opened the door.
- She took his hat and stick.
- He looked at the pictures on the wall.
- He tried to read a newspaper.
- The young woman came back.
- She led him into another room.
- The doctor said good morning to him.
- Mr Roy sat down in an armchair.
- The doctor stood near him.
- Mr Roy opened his mouth.
- The doctor pulled out three of his teeth.
- Mr Roy felt unhappy.
- A bird made a nest in this tree.
- It laid five eggs.
- Tommy saw the nest.
- He climbed the tree.
- He held on to a branch with one hand.

- He took two of the eggs.
- He put them in his mouth.
- He needed both his hands.
- He began to climb.

16.2. Improve your vocabulary

16.2.1. The following list contains some terms you have met in science. Use them in sentences to show you understand their meanings.

- Filter
- Evaporate
- Condense
- Expansion
- Dissolve
- Solution
- Metamorphosis
- Larva
- Pollinate
- Antennae

16.2.2. Use your dictionary to find a word that has the same meaning as the underlined words. The start of each required word has been provided.

The engine of the car has been taken to pieces. (dis…)

We watched as the workman knocked down the old house. (dem…)

He was arrested for spending forged bank notes. (coun…)

After the storm, the sports field was like a muddy swamp. (qua…)

We all gave some money towards the cost of the party. (con…)

Many San pictures painted on the walls have been discovered in the Karroo. (Mur…)

16.2.3. Use this idiomatic expression in sentences to illustrate their meanings.

- To keep something dark
- Turn a blind eye
- To beat about the bush
- To smell a rat
- Mind your P's and q's
- Make a bee line for

16.2.4. The endings of the following expressions have been muddled.

16.2.5. Re-arrange them correctly and use each expression in a sentence to show its meaning.

- Wear and ruin.
- Rack, and call.
- Fair and tear.
- Good and soul.

- Neck and sevens
- Heart and square.
- Head and crop
- Back and change
- Chop and shoulders
- Shoes and all.

16.3. Spelling

- Rule 2: When to drop the final silent e when adding a suffix.
- When adding a -y, or an ending beginning with a vowel, drop the final -e:
  - scare – scary, scaring
  - love – loving
  - Notice – noticing
  - Cube – cubic
- **Note the following exceptions when ending follows a soft c or soft g:**
  - Noticeable
  - Serviceable
  - Manageable
  - Courageous
  - Gorgeous
  - Outrageous

16.3.1. Spelling Activity

Add -ing to the following words: practice, lace, release, service please, come

Add y to the following words: inflate, manage, courage, pose, desire, nerve

Unit 5
Present Perfect Tense

17. Affirmative Form

17.1. How to Use This Tense Correctly

This tense is used

- To tell us about something that began in the past and has continued up to the present, e.g.

Mr Kosani has taught English for the past 20 years. (This implies that he still teaches it)

- To show something that has just happened, e.g.

    They have just left. (meaning, not long ago)

17.1.1. Adverbs of Time

This tense is associated with the following adverbs of time:

- Now, e.g. Your father has now arrived.
- Just, e.g. He has just spoken.
- Already, e.g. I have already prepared breakfast. Please, come over.
- Never, e.g. We have never heard from them.
- Ever, e.g. Have you ever seen the rain?

- Since, e.g. He has been here since this morning.
- For, e.g. We have lived here for 120 years.

- **NOTE WELL:**

The present perfect tense is the most common tense in the English language. It is concerned with the completion of an action by a given time, NOT with the time when the action happened.

17.1.2. Structure of Present Perfect Tense

- Singular s + auxiliary "has" + past participle form of a verb, e.g. She/he has spoken.
- Plural s + auxiliary "have" + past participle form a verb, e.g. They/we have spoken.
- Subject I + auxiliary "have" + past participle form a verb, e.g. I have spoken.

17.1.3. Oral Activity

For students to master the correct use of this tense, it is necessary for a teacher to conduct oral activities. Give full answers:

1) X, open the door.

   What have you done?

   What has X just done?

2) Y, go to the door.

   Where has she gone?

3) X, tell Y to "Go to your place".

What have you just told Y?

What have you done, Y?

4) X, shut the window. What have you done?

5) (Teacher drops the duster) What have I done?

6) (Teacher picks up duster and puts it on the table) What have I done?

7) X, Write your name on the board. What is he doing? What has he done?

8) Y, walk slowly to the door. What is she doing? What has she done?

9) X, say to Y to "Stay at the door".

10) Teacher throws chalk at X and asks, "X, read the first three sentences on page 8." What is he doing? What have you done, X? What has he done?

11) Y, give X your exercise book. What have you given her? What has she written on page 7?

12) Have you done any homework for me today?

13) Y, have you been to the cinema this week?

14) Have you ever eaten apple-pie?

17.1.4. Oral activity

- Give short-form answers, e.g.

Have you seen him?

No, I haven't,

or

Yes, I have.

1) Have you been to the zoo?
2) Have you lived here all your life?
3) Has X read to me today?
4) Have you had your breakfast?
5) Have you learnt perfect tenses before?
6) Has anyone cleaned the blackboard?
7) Have you done any homework this week?
8) Have you seen a good film recently?
9) Have you been up in a helicopter?
10) What good books have you read during the last few months?
11) Have you ever seen a hippopotamus?
12) Where have you put your pen?
13) Who has just gone out of the classroom?
14) Have you bought a new suit?
15) Have you done any work today?
16) Who has taken my pencil?
17) Have you left any books at home?
18) Why have you bought a two quire?
19) Has everybody understood everything about the correct usage of the present perfect tense?
20) Have you written down all these questions?

Nb: Correct Usage Of "Since" And "For" Regarding Present Perfect Tense

- "Since" denotes from some definite or period in the past till now.
- "For" denotes a length of time till now.

EXAMPLES

- "Since"

I haven't seen you since Monday

- "For"

I haven't seen you for a week.

17.1.5. Writing Activity

- Complete the following sentences with the given alternatives, e.g.:

1. I haven't seen you. (Christmas/three days)

    I haven't seen you since Christmas.

    I haven't seen you for three days.

2. We've been here. (an hour/January)

3. She hasn't spoken to me. (more than two years/last week).

4. They have lived in this street (1994/the last ten years/a long time)

5. I haven't had time to do it. (I was ill/last Monday)

6. We haven't bought any new ones. (a week/ages)

7. There hasn't been a famine here. (centuries/the middle ages)

8. I haven't eaten any meat. (I was a boy/over a year)

9. Nobody has written to me. (many weeks/my birthday)

10. You've asked the same question every day. (the beginning of the year/the last fortnight).

11. You haven't sent me any money. (last Saturday/fifteen days)

12. She has worn the same old dress. (at least a month/the beginning of month)

13. I haven't spoken Afrikaans. (1925/ten years).

14. 1 haven't ridden a bicycle. (longer than I can remember/my childhood)

15. It hasn't rained here. (more than a month/March)

Unit 6
Parts of Speech

18. Pronouns

Pronouns are words that take the place of nouns. They save clumsy repetition and they make the sentences read more smoothly. However, only use a pronoun when it is clear to which noun it refers or for which it stands.

18.1. Subjective Form and objective Form

Subjective *Form*	Objective Form
I	Me
He	Him
She	Her
We	Us
They	Them
You	You
It	It

- The subjective form of a pronoun is used as the subject of a sentence and the objective form of a pronoun is used as the object of a sentence e.g.

S	V	O
(1) Zola	Plays	With Lizo
He	Plays	With him
(2) Nomsa	Plays	With Thoko

She	Plays	With her

- The object, form of a pronoun is used AFTER a verb and preposition e.g.

Zola likes him.

Zola plays with me.

- "Than" is usually followed by the subject form of the pronoun e.g. Fie is older than I/he/she.

- When two or more pronouns are used together, and one of them is the first-person pronoun, the first-person pronoun is always named last e.g.

You and I will meet him. (not I and you) Both they and we have been invited. (not we and they)

- "Let" is followed by the objective form.

18.1.1. Practising Activity

- Choose the correct pronoun and rewrite the sentences.

1) (We/us) went with (they/them).

2) They knew all about my friend and (I/me).

3) Mr Jones and (he/him) came last night.

4) I came here with Jane and (her/she).

5) Basil gave Harry and (I/me) an ice cream, and then we went to the pictures with (he/him) and his friend.

6) He told Mary and (me/I) to go with (he/him) and his mother.

7) An old man asked my friend and (I/me) what the time was.

8) Go and see (he/him) and his friend.

9) There are same letters for you and (me/I).

10) Go with John and (her/she) to visit (they/them).

11) We're much stronger than (they/them) at football.

12) Let (we/us) all go for a walk except (she/her) since (she/him) is stronger than (I/me).

13) Do you think (he/him) is stronger than (I/me)?

14) How can you talk to a woman such as (she/her)?

15) It's only (I/me) and my friend.

16) Help (me/I) carry (she/her). (She/her) has fainted.

17) Nobody could answer except (I/me).

18) Let's go for a walk, just you and (I/me).

19) What! (I/me) accept a present from (they/them)?

20) I thought it was (they/them) who went with (she/her).

18.2. Possessive Pronouns

Possessive pronouns are: mine, yours, his, hers, ours, yours and theirs. They are substitutes of nouns that denote possession e.g.

- These pens are mine.
- That pen is yours.
- That book is his.
- Hers is the red car.
- It is the big kennel.

- Ours is already packed.
- Yours have still to be packed.
- Theirs have been dispatched.

The following are possessive adjectives that serve a descriptive function as well as indicating possession:

- These are my pen.
- That is her book
- Those are his books.
- These are our books.
- This is their classroom.
- This is your pen.
- These are your pens.
- Its tail is bushy.

Possessive adjectives are: my, her, his, our, their, your, (Singular), your (plural) and its (for things or animals).

18.3. Fill in the correct pronouns by re-writing the whole sentence.

1) This pen is………….. I bought it yesterday.
2) I like…………handwriting. …………..is legible than…………….
3) Please be careful………blades are very sharp.
4) I cut…………with a knife the other day.

5) It's…………they bought it………….

6) We enjoyed…………very much at picnic.

7) She has been made very famous by………. her dedication to the entertainment industry.

8) I don't think she'll be able to manage by…………….

9) Why is Zola sitting here all by……………in the dark?

10) You must look after………on……….trip to Pilgrims' Rest.

11) Joe says the hat is not……, although it's just like the one he bought……… last week.

12) He must remember to behave……….in ……….own place just as well in other peoples.

13) I always have to remind……that this book is and not……one day I'll take it away with……….own book.

14) Have we got to do it all by………….?

15) This book is………….I wrote………….name in it…………….

16) This doesn't look like……….book, it must be……………….

17) Tell him not to forget………..ticket, she mustn't forget…………either.

18) Tell me, isn't that………….old car over there?

19) It was very good chocolate, but I've eaten all……. can you give me a little piece of?

20) They have two of………….houses in this street, and the house on the corner is also………….

21) I see that he has lost………….pencil, perhaps you can lend him………….

22) ………….is a very bad one…….what's like?

23) You can take………and give me…………….

24) Zola has come to see me,………….father and…………were school friends.

25) We've taken………share, has she taken …………….?

26) I saw a procession of……….in the street this morning.

27) You said you would introduce me to a friend of……….who had a car to sell.

28) He wants………. to return a book you borrowed last week.

29) They told me to call on a friend of in ………..Cape Town.

30) An aunt of…………….has just crashed his car on the highway.

18.4. Demonstrative Pronouns

These pronouns point to someone or something. They are:

This (singular) and

These (plural) refer to something or someone nearby,

That (singular) and those (plural) refer to something or someone further away.

18.5. Interrogative Pronouns

Interrogative pronouns are:
- Who
- Whose
- Whom
- What
- Which

These pronouns are used for the purpose of asking questions.

18.5.1. WHO AND WHOM

These pronouns are used only when the questions refer to persons.

"Who" is used when it stands in the place of a noun used as the subject of a sentence.

"Whom" is the form used when the noun for it is substituted is used as an object:

Who asked you? (subject of asked)

Whom did you see? (object of did see)

18.5.2. WHICH

"Which" relates to places and things as a rule. Sometimes it may relate to persons:

- Which do you prefer?
- Which of the players would you choose?

18.5.3. WHAT

"What" refers to things in general, whereas "which" has a more restricted meaning:

- What is the matter? (general)
- Which is the one you mentioned? (restricted)

18.5.4. WHOSE

"Whose" is the possessive form of "who" and is used when possession is denoted.

- Whose is this pen? (that is, who owns it)

18.5.5. Practising Activity

- Add an interrogative pronoun to the following questions:

1. ……….is your name?
2. ………..is that pretty girl?
3. …………..is your telephone number?
4. Here are the books………is yours?
5. ……….is coming to tea?
6. ……….trees grow in desert?
7. ……………is yours, the orange or mango?
8. …………colour is it?
9. ………….makes your shoes?
10. …………..makes tea sweet?
11. ………….wants a piece of bread?
12. ………….piece of bread is yours?
13. ………….is the name of your bakery?
14. ………….is his shop, the one at the end of the road, or the one near the post office?
15. ………..understands this activity?
16. …………..of you understand this exercise?

17..............is the answer to my questions?

18................knows the answer?

19.............teaches you English?

20.............. are you learning now?

18.6. RELATIVE PRONOUNS

They are:

- Who
- Whom
- Whose
- Which
- That

The relative pronoun introduces a subordinate clause and refers to a noun in the main clause:

- This is the man who wrote the novel.
- She is an actress of whom we shall still hear a great deal.

- **NOTE WELL**

The object form occur after prepositions

- This is the boy to whom I gave my order.

"Whose" indicates possessions:

- The man whose shop was robbed died of heart attack today.

18.6.1. Practising Activity

- Add the relative pronouns in the blank spaces e.g. The man who spoke with me at the church was my cousin.

1) The book_____ I was reading yesterday was a detective story.

2) The man_____ you spoke to in the street is my English teacher.

3) I would like to see the trees_____ you picked these apples from.

4) There's the lady_____ purse has been stolen.

5) The people_____ you were living with in Pretoria are coming to see you.

6) The painting _____ you were talking about has been sold.

7) People_____ live in glass houses shouldn't throw stones.

8) Buy it back from the man_____ you sold it to.

9) What's the name of that man _____ wife has been away?

10) Can you remember the person _____ you took it from?

11) Where is the shop sells picture – postcards?

12) That's the knife and fork_____ I eat with.

13) Where is the man_____ who sold me these sun-glasses?

14) What's that music_____ you are listening to?

15) I don't like the house_____ he lives in.

16) The man_____ made these shoes doesn't know his trade.

17) Here comes the girl_____ I am hiding from.

18) The people are_____ looking at that house are my parents.

19) The house_____ they are looking at is my house.

20) And the girl_____ you see at the door is my sister.

21) The paint on the seat_____ you are sitting on is still wet.

22) The shirts_____ Simeon wears are classic.

23) Any man_____ who listens to you is a fool.

24) The old gentleman_____ lives across the road has got married for the fifth time.

25) The lady_____ you were speaking to just now jilted her boyfriend at the party last night.

18.7. Indefinite and General Pronouns

These pronouns do not refer to any particular person, thing, class, amount, weight, number and the like:

- Some, someone, somebody, something,
- Any, anyone, anybody, anything,
- Every, everyone, everybody,
- No one, none, nobody, nothing,
- Other, another, others,
- Each, each one
- One
- All
- Both

- Either
- Neither

18.7.1. PRACTISING ACTIVITY

* Add the correct indefinite or general pronouns in the blank spaces:

a) ……….. some make it,………..do not.

b) ……….. came knocking at my door.

c) ……….. was troubling him.

d) There are……… ways of doing it.

e) Can you think of ……….way of doing it?

f) ……….. man, strong enough may challenge the champion.

g) …………. with dirty hands should not serve food.

h) …………….who knows about the crime should contact crime stop.

i) …………. of the men is willing to do this duty.

j) ………... of them were dismissed for incompetent performance.

k) ………….. knows this answer or that answer is wrong.

l) …………….Peter nor Ken is present.

18.8. Reading and Reasoning Activity

- Read this passage entitled The Family Tree silently before you answer in full sentences all questions based on the passage.

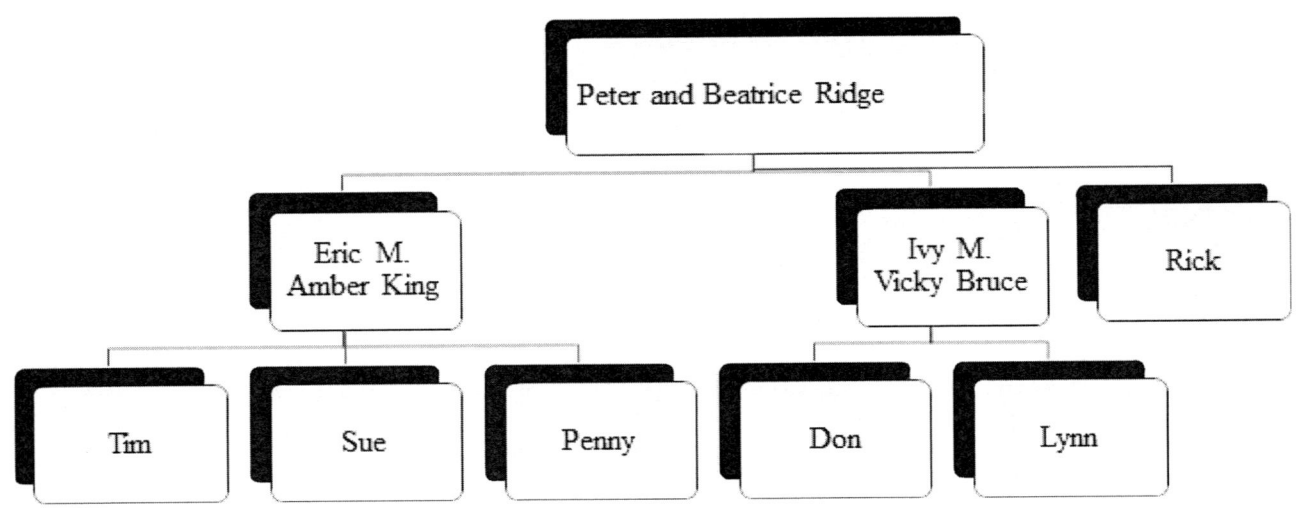

- **NOTE WELL**

M stands for married

1. Who are the children of Peter and Beatrice Ridge?
2. Whom did Eric and Ivy marry?
3. Who is the bachelor among the children of peter Ridge?
4. Who is Rick's brother-in-law?
5. Who is Ivy's sister-in-law?
6. Who is the son-in-law of Peter Ridge?
7. Who is the mother-in-law of Amber King?
8. Who is Tim's uncle?
9. Who is Penny's aunt?
10. Who are Rick's nephews?
11. Who is Eric's niece?

12. Who are the grandchildren of Peter and Beatrice Ridge?

13. What is the maiden name of Don's mother?

14. What is the surname of Don and Lynn?

15. What is the surname of Tim, Sue and Penny?

Question 1 (b)

Now draw your own family tree. Go back as far as your great-grandfather and great-grandmother.

Question 1

State the wedding anniversary that Peter and Beatrice Ridge would celebrate on the

i. 25th year

ii. 50th year

iii. 60th year

iv. 100th year

Unit 7
Present Perfect Tense

19. Negative Form and Question Form

19.1. Answer the following questions in the negative form:

1) Have you been to the zoo?
2) Has she lived here since her childhood?
3) Has Tom read the book today?
4) Have they had their breakfast yet?
5) Have you done your homework?
6) Has he bought a new car?
7) Has Themba understood everything about the present perfect tense?
8) Has the dog chased the thief away?
9) Have you seen a good film recently?
10) Have you spoken Greek since the beginning of this year?

19.2. Ask questions by simple inversion.

For example:

He has gone to town. (statement)

Has he gone to town? (question)

1) They have lived in this area for generation.

2) I have seen you for three days.

3) She's bought new clothes for the occasion.

4) There has been drought here for the past three years.

5) I've eaten my breakfast.

6) She has written to me for my birthday.

7) She's worn that jacket since the beginning of the month.

8) I've spoken Greek for ten years.

9) It has cost a lot of money.

10) You've torn your coat.

19.3. Future Perfect Tense

19.3.1. How to Use This Tense Correctly

This tense is used to express a certain action that will be completed by a certain future time.

- The completion of the action is what interests us. NOT the time of the action itself, for example:

1) I shall have played five songs of the West Life by 3 O'clock.

- This tense also tells us about something that it is assumed has been completed before another begins for example:

2) I'm sure that you will have read book.

19.3.2. Practising Activity

In two paragraphs, explain what you will have achieved by the time you are forty years.

19.4. Past Perfect Tense

19.4.1. How to Use This Tense

This tense is used to show which of the two past actions happened first:

1) When I arrived at 6, the train had already left.

2) If you had explained it, I should have understood

- This tense is also used in reported speech to express the sequence of tenses, i.e. the past tense changes to the past perfect tense:

3) Peter told me, "We arrived at 6 on Friday." (Direct speech) Peter told me that they had arrived at 6 on Friday. (Indirect/reported speech)

19.4.2. Practising Activity

Give the correct form of the verbs in brackets by re-writing each sentence:

1) The aeroplane (arrive) by the time the sun (set).

2) He (discover) to his horror that he (eat) half a maggot with his last piece of apple.

3) A friend of mine once (write) a chilling story called Twilight Incidents of the Brothel, although he (never visit) a brothel in his life.

4) The little boy (ask) what (happen) to his skating-board.

5) The accused replied, I (come) at the party at 10 o'clock, not at 8 when the incident (take) place.

6) By the end of seventeenth century large numbers of the French (come) to Cape.

7) John Lennon (become) famous as the rock star before his thirtieth birthday.

8) He (cannot) help thinking that he (see) that face somewhere before.

9) After he (be) taken to see Timeless Citadel he (tell) all his friend that he (never see) a better opera.

10) His father (worry) a lot about him before she (hear) that he was safe.

11) The politician (declare) that his party always (stand) for social security.

12) Before Verwoerd (come) to South Africa; he (live) in the Netherlands.

13) There (be) several robberies in that street before the municipality (provide) street lights.

14) By the time John (finish) his meal, it (be) seven o'clock.

15) The house (be) much smaller than he (think) at first.

16) The historian (say) that the power and the glory of the pharaohs of the ancient Egypt (not be) at all far-fetched.

17) The valley (flood) the year before and so it (contain) plenty of green, pasturage.

18) It (be) the hardened criminal who (do) the killing.

19) He jumped up and down as if he (possessed).

20) He (know) of only one tiger that was kept as a pet; and it (never show) a trace of ill temper.

19.4.3. In five sentences, state all the things you had done by 7 last night.

Begin each sentence like this:

By 7 last night, I…

19.5. Improve Your Vocabulary

19.5.1. Match the proverbs in Column A with their meanings in Column B

A	B
(a) Absence makes the heart grow fonder	A well-dressed person may be taken for someone important.
(b) A friend in need is a friend indeed	One person has the same right to fair treatment as any other.
(c) Necessity knows no law	Overconfidence leads to mistake
(d) Procrastination is the thief of time	Affection is greater when someone is not present
(e) What is sauce for the goose is sauce for the gander	When something is essential, legal rights do not count
(f) Self-praise is no recommendation	If you delay, you may lose your opportunities
(g) Pride goes before a fall	Anyone can speak well of himself
(h) Fine feathers make fine birds	Anyone who helps you when you are in difficulties is a true friend.

19.5.2. Pair off the idiomatic expressions in column A with their meanings in column B.

(a) cut and run	Refuse to listen
(b) call in question	Face difficulties resolutely
(c) take the bull by the horns	To be similar to
(d) bear out	Tie between two competitors in a race

(e) bear resemblance	Constantly change one's opinions
(f) dead heat	Go away quickly
(g) turn a deaf ear	Prove
(h) blow hot and cold	Say that one is doubtful about something that appears to be true.

19.6. Possessive Case

It is indicated by the apostrophe "s" and it means that someone owns something

1) The book of Peter.
2) Peter's books (possessive case)

19.6.1. Rules for the Correct Use of the Apostrophe

A.   If the Noun is singular; add only "'s":

(1) A cap of a boy > a boy's cap.

B.   When the Noun is in the plural and ends in "s", add only the apostrophe after the "s".

(2) Caps of the boys > boys' caps.

C.   When the noun is in the plural and does not end in "s", add only "'s".

(3) Hats of men > men's hats.

D.   When using the apostrophe with surnames ending in "s" add "'s".

(4) The house of Mr Charles > Charles's house.

E.   Some phrases that begin with "for", "of a", "of the" may also take the possessive form:

(5) Leave for a month > a month's leave

(6) Greetings of the season > the season's greetings.

(7) The work of one day > one day's work.

F. In the case of double names, use the apostrophe with the last name:

(8) The shop of Jill and Peter > Jill and Peter's shop

19.6.2. Practising Activity

- Put into the possessive

(1) The father of James.

(2) The book of the boy.

(3) The bags of the ladies.

(4) The desks of pupils.

(5) The tools of the workmen.

(6) The car of Mr Edwards

(7) The typist of Mr Sims

(8) The new tie of my friend Cyril.

(9) The work of a whole day.

(10) The birthday of the president of South Africa.

(11) The parents of all the other boys.

(12) The famous shop of Fortein and Myburg

(13) The houses of Henry and Mr Jones.

(14) A wrist-watch of a lady or gentleman.

(15) He's the favourite of the boss.

19.7. Reading and Reasoning Activity

THE FUGITIVE

There he stood, a complete stranger, in their own sitting-room.

"Come in and sit down," he said, quite pleasantly, then added grimly, when they were seated, "stay there!"

"Who are you?" asked Don, in rather a shaky voice.

"That needn't concern you," replied the stranger. "Just behave yourselves and you'll be all right."

He was well-dressed, the children noticed, but he looked dirty and unshaven. Mum and Dad would not be home for an hour or so. They were visiting friends, so Don and Penny had gone to the cinema and returned home at 9 pm only to meet with this unexpected and frightening reception.

There's something familiar about his clothes, thought Penny, as she sat still not daring to move. "That's Dad's suit!" she suddenly called out, as she realised the truth.

"Was Dad's suit, you mean," said their strange guest. "I've left him mine." He pointed to a comer, and Don, seeing what was there, gasped in dismay.

"You're a convict."

"Clever boy," said the man, walking to the front door. He turned the key in the lock and calmly put it his pocket.

"I'm afraid I must go."

He went through the kitchen, opened the back door, removed the key to the outside and stepped out into the darkness. They could hear him locking it too, and then the crunching of his feet on the gravel path. At that time there was a sudden uproar. A long, drawn-out growl was followed by a startled curse. Don dashed to the kitchen window.

"Giants got him!" he shouted excitedly to his sister. "Quick, telephone the police."

When the men in blue arrived five minutes later, the intruder was still there. He dared not move. How could he, when he was lying on his back, the bared fangs of a huge Alsatian a few centimetres from his face?

19.7.1. How Well Did You Understand the Passage?

- Answer all questions in full sentence.

1. At what time of the day did the event take place?
2. Where had Don and Penny been up till then?
3. What warning did the stranger give them when seated?
4. Why did Don address the man "in a rather shaky voice"?
5. Why did the children not shout to their parents for help?
6. How do you think the stranger was dressed before he broke into their home?
7. How did he make sure of his escape?
8. Why did the stranger make a startled curse?
9. How many characters are in this story?
10. Which one is (a) the villain, (b) the hero: Don, Penny, Giant, the fugitive?

19.7.2. How Many New Words Did You Learn?

Find the word in the passage with this meaning:

1. An unknown person.
2. One who flees from justice.
3. To take short quick breaths.

4. Not having shaved.
5. Easily known or recognised.
6. A long-term prisoner.
7. A certain breed of dog.
8. A visitor.

19.8. Punctuation

- Punctuation is used in writing to clarify meaning of a sentence.

19.8.1. Capital Letters

- The first letter of a word is a capital when:
  1) It is at the beginning of a sentence:
- Shiba wants to be proficient in English.
  2) When it is a proper noun or a proper adjective:
- South Africa: Nelson Mandela; Friday; January; Australian mutton.
  3) When it is at the beginning of a sentence of direct speech:
- Jikijela exclaimed, "You are speaking my own language although UnguMlungu, we'll be friends as from today!
  4) When it is the first word of a private or business letter:
- Dear Uncle, My dear Tracy, Dear Sir/Madam.
  5) When
  6) "yours" is used at the end of a friendly or business letter:
- Yours sincerely, Yours faithfully. Yours affectionately, etc.

7) When it is a noun, adjective or pronoun referring to the Deity:

• God; the Supreme Being; The Holy Ghost; Him; He; Qamata; Mvelingqangi; Modimo; Allah; Jehova or Yahweh.

8) "I", is always written with a capital letter whenever it appears

19.8.2. Full Stop (.)

The full stop is used:

(a) At the end of all sentences, except direct questions or exclamations: He pointed to a comer.

(b) After an abbreviation or after initials:

A.A., B.A., doz., e.g., para., B.K. Kosani etc.

• The full stop is not used after the following because they are not strictly speaking abbreviations:

1st; 2nd; 3rd; 8th; percent.

19.8.3. Question Mark (?)

• A question mark is asked at the end of a sentence that asks a direct question:

"Where is the ticket office, my friend?"

• A question mark is also used at the end of a sentence that implies a question:

"You are a Xhosa, then, umfundisi?

19.8.4. Commas (,)

The comma is not that difficult to use correctly. A comma in the wrong place or the omission of comma can completely change the meaning of a sentence. Tire following rules are essential in the correct use of a comma:

1. A comma is used to separate words and phrases in a series:

- The ingredients you need to make the cake are sugar, butter, milk, flour and currants.

- He works morning, noon and night.

- I asked him a month ago, two weeks ago and yesterday.

2. A comma is used to separate words and phrases or clauses in apposition (that is, put side by side):

- Johannesburg, the largest city in South Africa, has a very pleasant climate.

- Joe, his sister, and Thandi, his cousin, are both coming.

3. A comma is generally used to mark off words and expressions such as: however, therefore, that is, intact, of course:

- You should, however, not forget what I have said.

- It is, in fact, not a very difficult problem.

4. A comma is often used to mark off a phrase that appears at the beginning of a sentence:

- The weather having improved, we decided to resume our journey.

- Having seen it once, I do not want to see it again.

19.8.5. Semi-Colon (;)

- A semi-colon marks a longer pause than that indicated by a comma. Its main uses are:

a) To separate the co-ordinate clauses of a compound or complex sentence, particularly when the conjunction is omitted;

- Go to the ant, thou sluggard, consider her ways and be wise.

b) To separate the co-ordinate clauses of a compound or complex sentence, especially when the sentences are long and a comma would not indicate a long enough pause:

- Soon after, Sir Benteiy Kirchoff's car came to the gate, and he drove away, but the chef held his peace that evening, and for many evenings to come.

19.8.6. Colon (:)

- The colon is used:

  a) To introduce a quotation or saying:

- Remember the proverb: 'Out of sight, out of mind'

  b) To introduce a list of facts:

- These are what you need: quickness, intelligence and sympathy.

  c) To separate two co-ordinate clauses when the second clause explains what is said in the first pail:

- I liked the idea: it was stimulating and helpful.

19.8.7. Brackets ()

- Brackets are used to enclose words that are not essential to the meaning of the sentence:
- That was the year (1948) when everything went wrong. When they did find out (and it was not easy), it was not really what they foresaw.

Note the comma after the bracket. A comma may follow, but never precede a bracket.

19.8.8. Dash (-)

- The dash is generally used to denote a sudden change of thought:
- Let me explain – but you may not be interested – what happened after you had left.

19.8.9. Exclamation Mark!

- An exclamation mark is used at the end of a sentence that expresses an emotion or feeling such as surprise or excitement:
- How frightened we were!
- I wish she were here!

19.8.10. Quotation Marks or Inverted Comas ("")

a)   Quotation marks, or inverted commas, are used to mark off the actual words used by a speaker:
- "I don't understand," he said.
- "Stop paddling," cried Jack suddenly. "I see it coming up behind us."

b)   They are also used in handwritten or typed matter to indicate the titles of books, plays, periodicals and the names of the ships:
- "I had an Owl Call my name"
- "Echoes of the Distant Oceans"
- "Sarah Baartman" (South African Ship)

19.8.11 Apostrophe (')

a) An apostrophe is used to show omission of letter or letters:
- Can't (short form of cannot)

b) It is used to show omission of numbers:
- '94 (short form of 1994)

c) It denotes possessive case:
- Boy's bedroom
- Boy's hostel

19.8.12. Ellipsis (…)

- It is used to indicate a deletion, usually to avoid a lengthy quotation:

    e.g. In his keynote address he quoted from "Elegy written on a country Churchyard", the following line "Full many a flower…"

19.8.13. Practising Activity

- Punctuate correctly the following:

Look here young fellow cried the angry farmer what are you doing up there in my apple tree please sir replied the boy one of your apples fell down and I'm trying to hang up

Unit 8
Simple Future Tense

20.1. How to Use This Tense Correctly

a) The simple future tense is used to express a future time or a future intention:

- He will pay me on Friday.
- I shall tell him what has happened.

b) It is also used to express a promise, willingness, a determination, certainty or a threat:

- He shall pay me on Friday. (certainty)
- I will tell him what has happened. (promise, determination or threat)

20.2. Adverbs of Time

- This tense is indicated by the following adverbs of time:
- tomorrow:
  i. I shall go home tomorrow. (simple future)
  ii. I will go home tomorrow. (determination)
- NEXT
  iii. We shall arrive next Friday. (simple future)
  iv. We will arrive next Friday. (determination)

20.3. Points to Keep in Mind About the Use of Simple Future Tense

- "Shall" is used with the first-person pronouns "I" and "We" to express a future time or a future intention without determination, certainty, promise or threat:

    i. I shall win the game.

    ii. We shall win the game.

- "Will" is used with the pronouns: he, she, they, you, it and nouns to express a future time or a future intention without determination, certainty, promise or threat:

    iii. He/she/they/you/Themba/Nomsa/the children/you/it will win the game.

- The roles of "shall" and 'will' are reversed in the light of the above rules in order to express a promise, willingness, determination, certainty or threat ;

    iv. By hook or by crook, I will win the game!

    v. We will win whether you like it or not!

    vi. By hook or by crook, he/she/they/you shall win!

20.4. Practising the Correct Use of Simple Future Tense

A.   Complete these sentences by using shall or will

a) I hope that you…….be able to come.

b) The sun……set at seven o'clock.

c) I am sure that he……find this book useful.

d) I think that she………be here this evening.

e) I do hope that it……….be fine on Sunday.

f) No unauthorised person…….enter these premises.

g) We are sure that they.......succeed.

h) Zola.........be sixteen on Wednesday.

i) The manager has promised that he......open the shop next Monday.

j) Take my word, you.........have it ready this afternoon.

B. In each of the following sentences say whether "shall" or "will" expresses:

i. pure futurity

ii. a promise

iii. a determination

iv. a threat, or a combination of more than one of them:

a) They shall suffer for this.

b) Do hurry or you will be late.

c) Let's hope that we shall be able to sell it.

d) I will see her Friday.

e) Do you think that he will lend you the money?

f) We expect that we shall see him.

g) Not one penny will I give him.

h) Ladies and gentlemen, the meeting shall begin at ten o'clock.

i) You will find it a difficult problem at first glance.

j) I will get in touch with him as soon as I can.

20.5. Other Ways of Expressing a Future Idea

- A future idea is also conveyed by verbs such as:

i. are to:

They are to act as they are ordered.

ii. choose:

He does not choose to take leave.

iii. going to:

He is going to depart tomorrow.

iv. Intend:

They intend to form a new party next year.

v. like:

Would he like to accompany us to the seminar?

vi. mean:

What does he mean to do this evening?

vii. promise:

We promise to offer you what you have asked for, nothing else.

viii. refuse:

I refuse to obey your orders. I nearly incriminated myself today.

ix. want:

Do you want to go with me tomorrow?

20.5.1. Use future substitute forms where possible in the following sentences:

a) They (go) where they like.

b) I (ask) them where they are staying.

c) You (stay) with us this summer?

d) They not (take) the present.

e) She (cancel) the ticket.

f) He not (buy) his shoes there anymore.

g) They (return) to Sandton in a month's time.

h) I (pass) my exam.

i) You (come) with me to the party tonight.

j) You (do) as you are told!

20.6. Reading and Reasoning Activity

Mistakes Winners Don't Make

I've watched successful people at work and at play – Ron Perelman, billionaire owner of Revlon, actors, such as Nicholas Cage who've struggled to the top. But I also know many who haven't made it – shinning stars from universities who sell shirts, computer hotshots who deliver pizzas, and Maths geniuses who fix pipes in rotting blocks of flats.

Why do many people have the intelligence to succeed but never do? Of course luck has a role. But usually people make their own bad luck by regularly getting trapped in self-defeating attitudes and shoot-yourself-in-the-foot behaviour.

Here are some of the eight habits of really unsuccessful people one must avoid:

1. Delusional thinking.

   Unsuccessful people constantly lie to themselves about their own lives. They are dishonest to themselves about where they are in life, and what their prospects are for achieving goals. For example, my neighbour who teaches art apart time craves for the middle-class lifestyle. She can't seem to understand why teaching part time won't pay a living wage.

2. Not producing.

   I've repeatedly talked to people who fail to acquire any useful skill for which someone will pay real money. They don't understand the fundamental truth that persons get paid for being able to do something that adds a lot of value.

That means medicine or law or song writing or finance or something that will help others to get well or make money or enjoy themselves or learn something on a big scale.

My father taught me that all rewards in life accrue to either financial capital or human capital. Financial capital is often inherited. One has no control over that. Human capital, a marketable skill, can be acquired only through training and effort.

Unsuccessful people can spend their whole lives evading this truth.

3. Punishing friends

Unsuccessful people have a habit of being friendly and grateful to those who are unhelpful to them, and disdainful and ungrateful to those who are kind to them.

Losers take their friends for granted at their own disadvantage, unless you are a uniquely talented person. You cannot succeed without a network of friends and supports. The inability to make and keep friends is the characteristic of failure

4. Bad manners

Unsuccessful people are also routinely rude. They fail to arrive on time to thank givers for gifts and to apologise for slights and wrongs. According to a success/lateness standard, a guest with a good job, extremely busy, with huge responsibilities will be on time. Someone with nothing to do all day will be very, very late or maybe not arrive at all. Someone with a low-level job will arrive between 15 minutes and an hour later.

One of my friends had a promising career as a producer. As time went by, his career began to falter and his decline was aided by his amazing lack of manners

5. Dressing for failure

Unsuccessful people habitually dress inappropriately. They arrive for job interviews without a tie or in running shoes. They come to dinner parties in jeans when everyone else is in suit. They may think they're making a fashion statement. Actually they're making a visual statement that they don't belong where they are, and that they have contempt for the people who do.

6. Bad attitudes

The unsuccessful often have a sour, pessimistic outlook. They dislike their work and assume that everyone around them is dishonest or stupid. Their own despair and hopelessness negatively infect the people around them. They also betray a lack of confidence in themselves, a deep-rooted belief that they can't do much or do it well. By doing so, they don't realise that they are advertising themselves as losers. They always bad mouths their bosses or their jobs. As a result they can't get any good reference from anyone they've worked for. It's a chronicled fate for chronicled complainers.

7. Needless arguing

Unsuccessful people like to argue just for the sake of argument. They may think that friends and colleagues will be impressed with how clever they are. They couldn't be more mistaken. However, this doesn't mean that you have to agree with everything anyone else say. But you can't annoy other people endlessly and still expect them to help you.

People who get things done don't like to spend their time arguing needlessly.

8. Putting first things last

Unsuccessful people cannot set priorities. If you tell them to do something, they will tell you they don't have enough time. The truth is there's never enough time to do everything, even everything of genuine importance. Unsuccessful people, however, never quite learn that setting priorities is an ironclad necessity. They also never seem to learn that it's not a sacrifice but a bargain to give up things of lesser- importance for those things of greater importance.

Adapted from the article by Benjamin Stein: Reader's Digest. January 1995

20.6.1. How Well Did You Understand the Passage?

- Always answer in full sentences in order to develop your proficiency in English.

- Do not transcribe the passage unless you have been asked to quote from the passage.

1. What has made Ron Perelman successful?
2. Briefly explain why some intelligent people fail to succeed?
3. Mention two things that constitute the fundamental truth, about being successful.
4. Briefly explain how the network of friends and supporters may help a talented person to succeed in life.
5. Mention at least three characteristics of bad mannered people.
6. State how tire success/lateness standard differentiate the successful from the unsuccessful.
7. Why is it proper to dress appropriately for job interviews and other occasions?
8. Sate any two results that occur as the consequence of bad attitudes in the work environment.
9. What is the basic negative impact of needless arguing?
10. Give an example that illustrates the expression: Putting first things last.

20.6.2. Enrich Your Vocabulary

• Without discouraging the use of a dictionary to check new words, at this stage of your studies you are advised to guess the meaning of a new word from the context, that is, the words that come before and go after it. To do so enables you to read fairly quickly.

• Answer by either filling in the missing words or by making a full sentence or by giving one word answer when asked to do so:

1. A billionaire of USA owns assets that are worth………dollars.
2. Computer hotshots are persons who are…………in using computers.
3. One's prospects are one's………goals or expectations.

4. Give an example of a fundamental truth.

5. How can a person get financial capital if a person has not inherited it?

6. Give an example of human capital as a marketable skill.

7. What does a disdainful person do which a grateful person does not do to his friends?

8. How does a pessimistic person view life?

9. How often do chronicled complainers complain?

10. Where often do you find colleagues?

20.7. Improve Your Vocabulary

A. Match the proverbs in Column A with their meanings in Column B and then write sentences that illustrate the meanings of the proverbs:

Column A	Column B
(a) As you make your bed, so you must lie on it.	You must test something before you can say whether it is good or bad.
(b) Blood is thicker than water.	When to know something makes one unhappy, it is better not to know it.
(c) God tempers the wind to the shorn lamb.	One must take the responsibility for one's own actions.
(d) Where ignorance is bliss, 'tis folly to be wise.	He must indeed be miserable if he can never enjoy himself.
(e) The proof of the pudding is in the eating.	The ties of relationship are stronger than those of friendship.
(f) Fools rush in where angels fear to tread.	Life is made easier for those who have suffered misfortunes.

| (g) It is poor heart that never rejoices. | There is always time in which to reform and improve one's conduct. |

B. Give one word for the underlined phrases and clauses:

   i. The bus arrived at the correct time.

   ii. The tramp went from door to door asking for food.

   iii. The hunters came towards the lions cautiously.

   iv. Although it was already late, we did not give up hope.

   v. This dress is too short. It will have to be made longer.

C. Replace the verb "said" by choosing the right verb from these:

Whispered	Asked
Complained	Roared
Laughed	Pleaded
Shouted	Exclaimed

a) "Come out of the rain," said mother from the bedroom window.

b) "What a marvellous view!" said the mountaineer

c) "You sold me rotten eggs, yesterday," she said to the grocer.

d) "Please forgive me," said Joan in tears.

e) "What are eight mines?" said Miss Green.

f) "Stand at ease!" said the Sergeant Major to the troops.

g) "Don't make a noise," said Nurse Goodman softly.

h) "What a funny joke," said Tubby almost in fits.

20.8. Punctuation

20.8.1. Punctuate the following passage correctly:

Hurray for the holidays we break up on the second of June cried Irene as they were packing their books yes ten more days of school and then three glorious weeks of freedom sighed Yvonne happily is it Saturday this week do we leave for Bushman's River asked Irene it is replied Yvonne and i cant wait till then

Unit 9
Future Continuous Tense

21.1. How to Use This Tense Correctly

This tense expresses what will be taking place at a particular future time:

- What will you be doing this time next week?
- By then I shall be revising my work in preparation for the exams.

21.2. Practising Activity

In five sentences, answer the following question:
What you will be doing in January next year?

21.3. Parts of Speech: Adjectives

21.3.1. What Is an Adjective?

An adjective is a word that describes a noun or a pronoun by giving us more information about the noun or pronoun:

a)   A strong man can push a tractor.

b)   He is strong to push a tractor.

- In the first sentences identify the adjective and the noun described by the adjective.
- In the second sentence identify the adjective that describes the pronoun.

21.3.2. Kinds of Adjectives

A.   Adjectives of quality:

1) big

2) fat

3) wide

4) high

5) long

6) broad

7) hard

8) sweet

9) red

10) black

11) tail

12) ugly

13) rough

14) old

15) soft

16) thick

17) heavy

18) clever

19) bright

20) slow

21) good

22) bad

23) far, etc.

B. Adjectives of quantity:

1) several

2) many

3) much

4) enough

5) little, etc.

C. Adjectives of number:

1) first

2) two

3) 3rd

4) few

5) many, etc.

D. Demonstrative adjectives

- They point out the things they describe by directing attention to them.

Singular	Plural
(1) This	(2) These
(3) That	(4) Those

- Do you like this book or do you prefer that book, over there?
- I don't prefer these books. Please give me those books over there.

E. Possessive Adjectives

- They are used to denote ownership.

Singular	Plural
1. my	2. our
3. his	4. their
4. her	5. their
6. its	7. their
8. your	9. your

F. Interrogative Adjectives

- Interrogative adjectives are used to ask questions Which or What:
- Which book would you like?
- What time do you expect him?

G. Distributive Adjectives

- Distributive adjectives show that the persons or things indicated by the noun which they qualify are to be considered singly or in separate lots: each, every, either, neither:

i. Each boy scored 60% in the exam.

ii. Every boy must wear full uniform.

iii. Choose either book.

iv. Neither student scored less than 40% in the exam.

H. Proper Adjectives

• Proper Adjectives are formed from proper nouns and must always begin with a capital letter:

(1) South Africa	South African
(2) Britain	British
(3) Congo	Congolese
(4) England	English, etc.

21.3.3. Position of adjectives in sentence

a) Except when it is used as the complement of a verb, an adjective usually precedes the noun that it describes:

- The blue book.
- The happy students.

b) When an adjective is used as the complement of a verb, it usually follows the verb:

- The book is blue.
- The students are happy.

c) If we want to emphasise an adjective, we may change the order of the words in the sentence, you will find many instances of this in poetry:

Bright and cool is the morning.

Instead of

The morning is bright and cool.

21.3.4. Practising Activity

a)   Name the kind of adjective in the following:

1. Tall plants	2. Less check	3. This torch
4. Enough money	5. Tenth place	6. Several books
7. Those onions	8. Red roses	9. Each day
10. Many friends	11. These guests	12. Short pants
13. Few cents	14. Much food	15. That man
16. Heavy loads	17. British car	18. My pen

b)   Write down the adjectives in these sentences and say which nouns they describe:

It was an immense task he had set himself.

1. To discover the routes he hoped to find would need many long and difficult journey through dense forest and dry country.

2. This lake was in the midst of swampy, fever-ridden country.

3. I have a vivid recollection of one occasion when a drive for duiker was in progress down a dry watercourse.

4. The second trip to Solomon's Mines was much more dangerous and difficult than the first.

5. When they wanted a new house, they cut down the green bamboo, thick as a man's hand, and stuck four poles into the ground.

6. Few as they were, they never surrendered their birth right.

7. Adonis dropped his eyes, trembling and blushing, as the wonderful lady spoke.

c) Give the proper adjective of the proper noun within brackets:

1. At the (China) restaurant we had (Mexico) chicken and rice.

2. Penelope has a (Siam) kitten and a (Scotland) terrier.

3. The (Japan) camera was as good as the (Canada) one.

4. (Denmark) bacon and (Holland) cheeses are famous.

5. I have a (Norway) car and a (Sweden) one.

21.3.5. Comparison of Adjectives

- There are three degrees of comparison, namely:

1. Positive:	This is the ordinary form of the adjective: old, young, tall, short, thick, thin etc.
2. Comparative	This is used only when two persons, things, animals or ideas are compared: •Joe is older than Zola.
3. Superlative	This is used when more than two persons, things, animals or ideas are compared. •Although Joe is older than Zola, Bholo is the oldest of the three

21.3.6. The rules for forming the comparative and superlative degrees from the positive degree of an adjective are as follows:

1) Where the adjective is a one or two syllable word we add -er to form the comparative and -est to form the superlative:

Old, older, the oldest

Tall, taller, the tallest

2) When the positive form ends in -e.

Only -r or -st is added:

Wide, wider, the widest.

3) When the positive ends in -y preceded by a consonant, the -y is changed to "i" before -er or -est is added:

Happy, happier, the happiest

Exception: shy, shyer, the shyest.

4) When the final letter of the positive form is a consonant, and this is preceded by a single vowel the last letter is doubled before -er or -est is added:

Fat, fatter, the fattest

Hot, hotter, the hottest

5) When the adjective has more than two syllables, we add "more/less" or "the most/least" before the positive form:

Helpful, more/less helpful, the most/least helpful

Foolish, more/less foolish, the most/least foolish

6) Adjectives with irregular comparative and superlative forms:

Positive Form	Comparative Form	Superlative Form
(i) good	Better	The best
(ii) bad	Worse	The worst
(iii) many	More	The most
(iv) much	More	The most
(v) little	Less	The least
(vi) far	Farther/further	The farthest/furthest
(vii) fore	Former	The foremost/first
(viii) late	Later/latter	The latest/last
(ix) old	Older/elder	The oldest/eldest

NOTE WELL:

a)   "Farther" means more distant, "further" also has the same meaning, but it also means "in addition" :

- Would you like to go any farther (or further?)
- Further, we must consider Bheki's point of view. (Not farther)

However, "farthest" and furthest" both mean the most distant:

At noon we reached the furthest or farthest point of the Mount Kilimanjaro.

b)   "Former" means the first of two things, and "latter" the second of two things. For more than two things, "first" and "last" are used :

- Of the two proposals I prefer the former.
- Of the two proposals I prefer the latter.
- Of all them I prefer the last.
- The tycoons drive the latest cars.

c)   "Less" is the opposite of "more" and is used with singular nouns. With plural nouns "fewer" is used, "more" is used with both singular and plural nouns

- Less effort
- Less noise
- Less work
- Fewer problems
- Fewer books
- Fewer pages
- More effort
- More noise

- More problems
- More books

d) "Elder" and the "eldest" refer to persons connected by relationship.

- My elder brother.
- Your eldest sister

Remember, you can say:

Zola is older than his sister.

You do not say: Zola is elder than his sister.

e) Some adjectives have no degrees of comparison because they are complete in themselves:

- Round, daily, weekly, double, square, middle, all.

21.3.7. Practising Activity

A. Complete these sentences:

a) Do you like this better that?

b) This coin is the (elder, eldest, older, oldest) of them all.

c) Who is the (oldest, eldest) of the three brothers?

d) John is (tall, taller, tallest) than either of them.

e) There were (little, less, least, fewer) spectators today than last week.

f) Of the two plans of action I prefer (later, latter, latest, last)

g) This house is (large, larger, largest) than our neighbour's.

h) Do you own the (last, latter, latest) cellphone in the market?

i) He is the (more, most) generous of them all.

j) The problem is (less, fewer, least) than we thought at first.

B. Study the results of this weekly test before you answer the questions based on the results:

Student	English	Math's	Accounting	Biology	Total
	50	50	50	50	200
1. Zola	22	30	24	38	114
2. Rita	26	28	35	32	121
3. Thembisa	24	32	22	30	108
4. Sisa	30	42	37	28	137
5. Thando	28	40	32	35	135
6. Rufus	32	35	40	45	152
7. Maisie	37	25	28	22	112
8. Xolani	40	37	32	25	134
9. Donovan	22	37	45	26	130
	261	306	295	281	

- Answer all questions in full sentences

  a) Who was the best student?

  b) In which subject were the most marks scored?

  c) In which subject were the fewest marks scored?

  d) Which subject was the most difficult?

  e) Who scored better marks in English than Maisie?

  f) Who scored more marks in Maths than Sisa?

  g) Who was the most hardworking student in Accounting?

  h) Which was the highest mark in Biology?

  i) Who obtained fewer marks in Biology than Maisie?

  j) Who scored the most marks in Biology?

21.3.8. Formation of Adjectives

- Here are some examples of the use of suffixes in the forming of adjectives:

Suffix	Example
(1) -able	Questionable
(2) -al	Emotional
(3) -(a) N	South African
(4) -ant	Pleasant
(5) -ary	Secondary
(6) -ate	Desperate
(7) -d	Baked
(8) -ed	Delighted
(9) -en	Wooden
(10) -ent	Dependent
(11) -ern	Northern
(12) -ful	Powerful
(13) -ible	Terrible
(14) -ic	Heroic
(15) -ing	Interesting
(16) -ish	Childish
(17) -ive	Attentive
(18) -less	Hopeless
(19) -like	Childlike
(20) -ly	Weekly
(21) -ous	Poisonous
(22) -some	Wholesome
(23) -worthy	Trustworthy
(24) -y	Needy

21.3.9. Practising Activity

A. Form adjectives by using once the following suffixes, and then use each of the adjectives that you have formed in sentences that illustrate their meanings:

- able
- al
- n
- ent
- ary
- ate
- d/-ed
- en
- ent
- ern

B. Form adjectives from these words by using suffixes other than - ing or -ed and then use each adjective with a suitable noun:

1. Success e.g. a successful plan
2. Exception
3. Time
4. Norway
5. Lament
6. Danger
7. Trouble
8. Leisure
9. Move

10. Italy
11. Enthusiasm
12. Supplement
13. Nature
14. Wonder
15. Sense
16. Sulphur
17. Help
18. Pity
19. Treachery
20. Year

C. From which words have the following adjectives been formed?

(1) Pleasant
(2) Desperate
(3) Terrible
(4) Attentive
(5) Apologetic
(6) Mischievous
(7) Numerous
(8) Private
(9) Characteristic
(10) Congratulatory

26.4. Punctuation

- Punctuate correctly

One morning Dr Winslow the famous novelist was taking prayers in his school presently a pupil saw a rat descending the bell-rope and burst out laughing later he was called to the office if you can think of anything tolerable to say Dr Winslow said I shall forgive you the troubling culprit addressed his master thus there was a rat for want of stairs came down a rope to go to prayers Winslow dropped the cane and gave the boy £1

21.4. Improve Your Vocabulary

21.4.1. Match the proverbs in Column A with their meanings in Column B

All is not gold that glitters.	A single example does not prove a case.
Easy come easy go	If you know in advance of a possible difficulty, you can take precaution.
One swallow does not make a summer	Appearances are deceptive.
Forewarned is forearmed.	Don't keep all your possessions in one place.
Dead men tell no tales.	Wait for problems to arise before you worry about them.
Bad excuse are worse than none.	The fact that we cannot have something makes it seem more attractive.
Every little helps	If a man is killed, he cannot give information about his murderer.
Forbidden fruit is sweetest	If many people give a little, a large sum may be collected
Do not meet trouble halfway	Defending ones conduct by giving a bad reason may lead to more trouble than giving no reason at all.

21.4.2. Match the idiomatic expressions in Column A with their meanings in Column B

Column A	Column B
Put the cart before the horse	Have a difficult task
A dark horse	Make brief
Cut short	Everything arranged
Have One's Work Cut Out	Do things in wrong order
Cut and Dried	Very quickly
By leaps and bunds	An unexpected winner

21.2.3. Choose the right word from the brackets and re-write the whole sentences

1. Pam is (laying, lying) down. She often (lays, lies) down.
2. I (advise, advice) you to practice, practise) daily.
3. The pills had no (affect, effect) on the patient.
4. Every car must have a (licence, license).
5. Pam refused to (except, accept) my apologies.
6. Our hens have (lain, laid, layed) many eggs,
7. Tom has been (lieing, lying) to his father.
8. Jill and Judy (lay, laid) awake all night.
9. Dr Green is a member of the (counsel, council).
10. (It's, Its) now useless. (It's, Its) lid is broken.

21.4. Adjective Phrases

- An adjective is a group of words in a sentence that describe a noun or a pronoun.
- A phrase is a group of words without a verb whereas a clause is a group of words which contains a verb, but one which is not the main verb of the sentence.
- Here are some examples of adjective phrases:

i. The boy on horseback is my cousin.

ii. He is a man of great ability.

iii. Did you meet the train from Durban?

iv. They live in a house with a thatched roof.

- The nouns that the phrases describe are "boy", "man", "train" and "house". These phrases, like adjectives, give us more information about the nouns that they describe. Without these phrases some of the sentences would be almost meaningless for example, "He is a man".

-

21.5.1. **Write down the adjective phrases in these sentences and say which noun or pronoun they describe:**

a) Please give me the magazine on that shelf.

b) Did you speak to the man at the bookstall?

c) We have to solve a problem of great difficulty.

d) They are enquiring about houses for sale.

e) He carried a few books on navigation.

f) Below that mountain lies the valley of the Nqweba River.

g) There was shade under the big tree near the new settlement.

21.5.2 Use each of these adjective's phrases in a suitable sentence, and underline the nouns or pronouns that they describe:

a) With three legs.

b) In the hand.

c) With a low ceiling.

d) In the next house.

e) With the name on it.

f) For the evening.

21.6. Reading and Reasoning Activity

The Cyclist's Road Safety Rules

1. KEEP WELL LEFT

    Always ride on the left edge of the road, thus allowing heavy traffic to overtake you safely. Keep a straight course. Avoid sudden swerves.

2. RIDE IN SINGLE FILE

    Two or more cyclists riding abreast occupy too much of the road for traffic to pass them and risk being knocked down by speeding cars.

3. DON'T WEAVE IN TRAFFIC

    When traffic is held up, keep your place and don't try to gain a forward position by "weaving" in the narrow spaces between stationary cars.

4. KEEP YOUR HEAD UP

    Keeping your head down may reduce wind resistance on the race track, but in traffic it is likely to produce a cracked skull.

5. BEWARE OF CAR DOORS

    When a car has stopped ahead of you, allow a fair margin in passing it, in case the driver or passenger suddenly open the door in your face.

6. HILLS

If a hill is so steep that you start wobbling before reaching the top, get off and walk. Control your speed downhill, otherwise you will find it impossible to stop quickly in a sudden emergency.

7. GIVE HAND SIGNALS IN GOOD TIME

Don't wait until the last moment. After signalling, return your hand to the handlebars before you actually start a right-turn.

8. KEEP BOTH HANDS ON THE HANDLEBARS

Don't "show off" by riding with your hands in your pockets, or your feet on the handlebars.

9. DON'T HITCH ON TO VEHICLES

It is dangerous to hold on to the side of a car or the back of a lorry.

10. DON'T CARRY PASSENGERS

A passenger sitting on the crossbar obstructs the rider's view and hampers control of the bicycle.

11. USE A CARRIER FOR PARCELS

Control of the bicycle is hampered by parcels in the hands. Put parcels or books in a carrier-basket, or on the rear baggage-carrier.

12. GIVE WAY TO PEDESTRIANS

Give old people plenty of space because they are slow, and children too because they are lively and unpredictable.

A. How Well Did You Understand the Passage

1. On which side of the road do all vehicles travel in South Africa?

2. Why must cyclists not ride two or more abreast?

3. Why is it dangerous for a cyclist to carry a passenger?

4. What is the rule when you want to turn right or left?

5. What risk do you take by pedalling with your head down?

6. Why must you be careful when a car stops ahead of you?

7. Why is it not safe to carry somebody on the crossbar?

8. What is meant by "weaving" in and out of traffic?

9. At night time what should you have at the back and front of your bicycle?

10. If you come to a stop sign, what should you do?

11. A robot has three coloured lights. Name them.

12. What does each of the three lights stand for?

13. When is the safest time to switch your bicycle lights?

14. Describe how you would give your bicycle a good overhaul.

B. How Many New Words Did You Learn?

1. What does a cyclist do when he/she does sudden swerves?

2. What is the difference between "stationary" and "stationery"?

3. Explain what does it mean "to produce a cracked skull"?

4. How does a cyclist ride when he wobbles?

5. Give the antonym of "down hill".

6. What is an emergency?

7. What does it mean to "show off"? Explain briefly.

8. Flow may a cyclist be hampered if a passenger is sitting on the crossbar?

9. What is the difference between a baggage and a luggage?

10. Explain how does an unpredictable event take place?

Unit 10
Parts of Speech

22. Prepositions

22.1. A preposition is a word that indicates the relationship of one thing to another. It is usually placed before a noun or pronoun in order to show how that noun or pronoun is situated.

A preposition may indicate

a) a spatial relationship:
- He is standing NEXT to me.
- The cat is UNDER the chair.

b) a source:
- Whiskey comes from Scotland.

c) Method
- By standing still, he hopes to remain unnoticed.

d) Time
- Students usually retire at 9 p.m.
- We study from Monday to Friday.
- He did well in the June exams.

e) mental or emotional attitudes :

- We are in love.
- Who is against us?

NOTE WELL: The only sure way of understanding the correct use of prepositions is to observe how they are used ordinarily and idiomatically.

22.2. The Common and the Most Common English Prepositions

- Here is the list of most common English prepositions:

    About, after, along, among, at, before, behind, beneath, between, by, down, for, from, in, in front of, into, like, near, next to, of, off, on, out of, over, past, round, since, though, till/until, to/towards, under, up, with, without.

- The common prepositions are:

    Above, across, against, below, beside, beyond, concerning, despite, except, inside, in spite, of, opposite, outside

- **Put In Suitable Prepositions:**

    1. We don't go……school……Sundays.
    2. Wait……me the……bus-stop.
    3. We arrived……Joburg…….exactly six o'clock.
    4. Come…….10…….Friday morning.
    5. I bought this hat…….R50.
    6. He hasn't been here……Monday.
    7. Our cat was bitten…….a dog.
    8. My home is…….Cape Town, but I was born……Dutywa, a small-town Eastern Cape.
    9. Put your books……the table.
    10. You may write…….pencil.

11. There's no bus, we'll have to go…….foot.

12. We went…….the seaside…….car.

13. Get……the bus here, and get off…….third stop.

14. Many planes fly…….the Atlantic nowadays.

15. We've been waiting………over an hour.

16. I'll call…….you…….a more convenient time.

17. Hold it carefully……your thumb and first finger.

18. I couldn't hear what they were talking…….They were speaking……… riddles.

19. A girl…….big eyes has just gone the door.

20. Here's a present…….you, don't forget it and go home…….it.

21. The teacher was sitting…….a desk……. the class.

22. ……him was a blackboard.

23. As he was coming…….me, he threw some orange…….peel the fence………his way…….the garden.

24. They were standing……. the two houses.

25. We had to go…….the hill…….a little house the top.

22.3. Improve Your Vocabulary

22.3.1. Write down the meaning of these proverbs, the meanings of which are given, but not in the same order:

a) Give a dog a bad name and hand him.

b) Discretion is the better part of valour.

c) Cut your coat according to your cloth.

d) Hope springs eternal in the human breast.

e) Too many cooks spoil the broth.

f) Every cloud has a silver lining.

g) Where there's a will, there's a way.

h) Two is company, three is none.

MEANINGS

a) Misfortune may be followed by happiness.

b) Live within your income.

c) When anyone has a bad reputation, it is difficult for him to get rid of it.

d) The intrusion of a third person is unwelcome.

e) Too many helpers are more likely to hinder than to help progress.

f) Do not be foolishly brave.

g) Even in the most desperate situation or most despairing moment, there is always the thought that the position will improve.

h) If one is sufficiently determined, obstacles are no barrier.

22.3.2. Match the idiomatic expressions in Column A with their meanings in Column B

Column A	Column B
(a) by fits and starts	Accept someone's views
(b) come into line	Make it impossible to change one's plans
(c) by hook or by crook	By spasmodic outburst of energy

(d) bum one's boats	Not based on facts
(e) be at someone's beck and call	By one means or another
(f) without foundation	Compelled to obey orders all the time

22.3.3. Use a word beginning with ex to complete these sentences:

a) Much damage was done before the fire was.......

b) Jason was fined for.......the speed limit.

c) My TV license....... on the 3rd of June.

d) George Pemba's paintings were....... in the Art Gallery of Port Elizabeth.

e) The miners were.......to great dangers underground.

f) Her son was.........from military service for unbecoming behaviour.

g) I....... my camera for a portable radio set.

h) South Africa.........fruit and wine to most of the countries of Europe.

i) Nancy is very.........with clothes and money.

j) The players were.......after a strenuous game.

22.3.4. Explain as clearly and as briefly as you can the difference between:

a) A gate and a door.

b) A fence and a hedge.

c) A carpet and a rug.

d) A desk and a table.

e) A dictionary and a directory.

f) A watch and a clock.

g) A chair and a bench.

h) A newspaper and a magazine.

i) An enquiry and an investigation.

j) An attorney and an advocate

22.4. Punctuation

Punctuate Correctly

Presently the donkey met a fox and the fox said hallo long ears why are you so sad then the donkey told him that he would like to have a beautiful Italian singing voice the fox who loved a joke said why that's easy enough all you have to do is practice really and truly asked the donkey as time and true replied the fox trying not to giggle you just practice for three months and youll be able to join the royal opera as bass

2.2.5. Reading and Reasoning Activity: Shark Hunting

Shark-Hunting

Ask a whaler which he'd rather face – whale or shark – and he would promptly grunt, "Neither!" But they don't call sharks "Tigers of the Deep" for nothing. For sea tigers they are. Cunning, blood thirsty, vicious and powerful as any tiger in the jungle. Sharks have appetites that has no power on earth or in the sea can satisfy. They swarm around whaling ships, and dart in to the attack when a harpooned whale is hauled alongside. And if they are not driven off with shots, they will tear the roped whale to ribbons.

Hunters and hunted – that's the shark: kill or be killed is its motto. No matter what comes along, a shark swallows it – an old saucepan flung overboard from some ships galley, a hundred kilogram turtle, porpoise, or even a man. You can catch this perfectly streamlined beast of the deep with and a hand-line and spear -if you are strong and lucky. But shark-hunters don't do that now. Easy enough to hook the savage fish but the hooked shark has got to be disabled and lugged aboard.

The hunters say a shark isn't dead until he's been skinned and cut up. That's their way of expressing distrust of a vicious fish that, to all appearances completely dead where it lies at the bottom of the boat, can snap a loose plank, or an oar, or a leg in two with one click of its razor-like teeth. So they don't leave captured sharks just lying about.

To make shark catching pay, you've got to do things in double-quick time. The shark-hunters go out with immensely strong nets, hundreds of meters long and six meters deep. They hang these nets upright in the sea, the tops buoyed up on the surface, lower and weighed with lumps of lead. No need to trouble about bait. Directly a shark jams its head between the strands of net, its fellows rush up to devour him and so more of them get their heads jammed.

More sharks dart to the fun until the seething net is hauled up. Shark-hunting is done just for fun. That sort of thing is too close to sudden death. It is done for a living, like whaling. Shark oil is valuable. So is the skin, for making boots and shoes, trunks and handbags. It is leather that won't wear out. They make walking sticks out of its backbone. And after they've tinned all the shark meat they want for human consumption; they make glue of what is left.

A.   How Well Did You Understand the Passage?

- Respond in full sentences to all questions;

1. Why are sharks deemed more dangerous than whale?
2. What sort of appetite is the shark reputed for?
3. Why are sharks very interested in the whaling ship?
4. What is supposed to be the shark' motto?
5. Why do shark-hunters distrust a hooked shark?
6. What modem method is used in the catching of sharks?
7. What type of bait do the shark-hunters use?
8. How are the nets held upright in the sea?
9. What is the approximate size of the shark-hunters' net?
10. How are the sharks caught by such a net?

11. Why shark-hunting is not done just for fun?
12. Quote the sentence that illustrates the sharpness of the shark's teeth?
13. When do shark-hunters consider hooked shark to be safe?
14. Why must the nets be immensely strong?
15. For what commercial purposes is the shark used?

B. How Many New Words Did You Learn?

1. The deep is another name for the……
2. Which four adjectives aptly describe the shark's nature?
3. How do sharks swarm around whaling ships?
4. Why a shark is referred to as the savage fish?
5. How are things done in double-quick time?
6. What is the opposite of "immensely"?
7. Which part of the ship is the galley?

For what is it used?

8. (Cruel, angry, fierce, wild) means the same as vicious.
9. The opposite of valuable is (invaluable, invalid, valueless)
10. If a plank is (lose, loose) it is not tight.

Unit 11
Parts of Speech

23. Adverbs, Adverb Phrases, Prepositions

23.1. Adverbs are words that describe more clearly a verb, an adjective, another adverb or adverb phrase:

- He walked slowly, (describing or modifying the adjective "impossible").
- It is an almost impossible task (modifying the adjective "impossible").
- We were too early (modifying another adverb "early").
- They arrived just in time (modifying adverb phrases "in time").

23.1.1. Kinds of Adverbs

a) Adverbs of time
  • They answer the question "when"
Now, soon, then, yesterday, tomorrow etc.

b) Adverbs of place
  • They answer the question "where"
Here, there, upstairs, inside, outside etc.

c) Adverbs of manner

- They answer the question "how"

Well, badly, slowly, quickly, carefully etc.

d) Adverbs of reason

- They answer the question "why"

Therefore, consequently, as a result etc.

e) Adverbs of degree

- They answer the question "to what extent"

Absolutely, almost, completely, considerably, entirely, greatly, immensely, much partly, rather, scarcely, thoroughly, quite.

f) Adverbs of frequency:

Always, already, continually, frequently, generally, hardly, just, never, nearly, occasionally, often, rarely, regularly, scarcely, seldom, sometimes, usually,

g) Adverbs of probability:

Doubtless, most likely, possibly, probably, unlikely.

h) Interrogative adverbs

How, when, where, why.

23.1.2. Adverb Position in a Sentence:

- Adverbs of time, place and manner are found at the end of a sentence.
    i. They left for Durban Yesterday.
    ii. He treated us carefully.

For emphasis, an adverb in this group is placed at the beginning of the sentence:

   iii. Yesterday they left for Durban.

- Adverbs of degree, frequency and probability are usually placed before the main verb, but after auxiliary verbs.

- The interrogative adverbs are found only at the beginning of the sentence.
- The adverbs of frequency and probability are usually placed after "is", are, was, were, should, would" :
    i.   He is always late at work.
- For emphasis they are placed before the verb:
    ii. He is always late at work.
- When there are two auxiliary verbs an adverb usually goes after the first one, except for an adverb of degree which usually goes after the second auxiliary:
    i.   Schools have often been disrupted this year.

ii. Schools have been considerably disrupted this year.

- Adverbs and adverb phrases usually follow the pattern:

Manner, place, time:

The councillors discussed the issue thoroughly in the conference last week.

23.1.3. Forming of Adverbs

- Most adverbs, especially adverbs of manner, are formed from adjectives:

1. By adding -ly:
    - Careful > carefully
    - Wise > wisely
    - Certain > certainly

2. By changing a "y" ending when it is preceded by a consonant to -ily:
    - Heavy > heavily
    - Satisfactory > satisfactorily

- Funny > funnily

3. By changing le ending to -ly:
   - Miserable > miserably
   - Possible > possibly

4. By adding s
   - Upward > upwards
   - Southward > southwards

5. By adding the suffix -wise:
   - Like > likewise
   - Other > otherwise etc.
   - Some adverbs have the same form as the corresponding adjective, other adverbs have a form of their own.

     Most adverbs, however, are formed by adding -ly to the adjective:
   - Adjective and adverb:

     Early, long, little, far, daily, monthly, enough.
   - Adverbs with a form of their own:

     Here, there, now, then, soon, thus, very, rather, seldom

NOTE WELL:

Not all words ending in -ly are adverbs.

These words are adjectives:

- Friendly, miserly, kindly, womanly, niggardly

If we wish to use such words as adverbs, we say:

- In a friendly manner,
- In a kindly manner

23.1.4. Adverb Phrases

An adverb phrase is a group of words beginning with a preposition. As its name implies an adverb phrase does the work of an adverb:

- We shall be here until five o'clock.
- Come after dinner.
- You'll find it on the table.
- Did you come by bus?

23.1.5. Practising Activity

A. For each of these phrases write down a suitable adverb:

Example: They'll be here in a few minutes.

They'll be here soon.

a) He drove without proper care.

b) At what time did he leave?

c) He'll be here in a short time.

d) To what place are you going?

e) We've been here for nearly three months.

f) We tried hard but without success.

g) Try to be there at exact time.

h) The train is three minutes behind schedule

i) I have not seen him of late.

j) You're five minutes before time.

B. Use these adverb phrases in sentences:

a) in the air

b) through the door

c) over the sea

d) to the park

e) at school

f) by airmail

g) in the front row

h) till midnight

i) before sunrise

j) about the town

C. Write down the adverbs or adverb phrases in these sentences and say which word or words they modify:

a) The noise could be heard distinctly.

b) It is too early to go yet.

c) Do you usually go in that direction?

d) He always speaks very briefly and to the point.

e) I have almost finished it, but not quite.

f) We cannot stay here long. We must leave in a few minutes.

g) You will find him in his office. He is always there at this time.

h) We often used to see them, but the never come to our house now.

D. Place the adverbs in brackets in suitable position in the following sentences:

a) I think she is diligent. (personally)

b) He wanted to leave the bequest to his youngest son. (originally)

c) It will be spring again. (soon)

d) I never saw her before. (actually)

e) They arrive before lunch. (generally)

f) We have to analyse how South Africa could alleviate rural poverty. (next)

g) They will take the morning bus. (possibly)

h) You could win the lotto if you play it thrice a week! (perhaps)

i) They found their lost luggage in the goods had. (luckily)

j) He has been visiting his ex-wife. (lately)

23.2. Put in suitable preposition

1. She was looking…….the window……the busy street.

2. We walked…….the main road, turned left…….the railway station, and went as far as the third turning…….the right.

3. Read…….line 10…….line 20…….page 27.

4. You can use my knife ……cut it.

5. The stream ran…….a little tunnel…….the roadway.

6. He spoke…….me…….his hands…….his pockets.

7. I walked…….one end of the street…….the other.

8. You can reach the station…….bus…….ten minutes.

9. The pictures will be shown…….one week longer.

10. I'm bringing an old book…….leather covers…….you this evening.

11. Don't look…….me like that!

12. A brick has fallen…….the well and knocked the bucket…….the rope.

13. I must look…….the postcard I got…….my teacher last week.

14. Most children remain…….school…….the ages of six and sixteen.

15. The first space shuttle travelled…….the world hundreds of times…….a few weeks.

16. I fell…….a rock when I was climbing…….a mountain last week.

17. It's further than I thought; it's…….ten kilometres…….the shortest route.

18. Switzerland lies………Germany, France and Italy.

19. I'm staying………friends not far the station.

20. Please come………me to the cinema tonight.

21. Who did you give the money………?

22. Children………four years………age do not often go school.

23. My school was founded………Chief Albert Luthuli in the 1960s.

24. Come and sit……this sunshade……a comfortable desk chair.

25. Do you want to speak………me………anything?

26. There's a knock…...the door. Who can be calling us ……… this late hour?

27. Don't go out………the rain………a hat.

28. I like to smoke a cigarette and listen……. the radio.

29. The cat is hiding………us………the table.

30. I must work hard…….pass Maths because I'm not very good…….it.

31. I wonder if I shall get…….my accounting examination.

32. You can cut the apple…….two……..this knife.

33. I go via the post office every day……my away…….work.

34. Let's go…….a walk…….the garden…….dinner.

35. When we get back……. our walk, we're going to sit…….. the fire …….half an hour.

22.3. Improve Your Vocabulary

A. The principal is the head of a school. What are the heads of these called?

1. A university
2. A newspaper
3. A hospital
4. A committee
5. A firm
6. A bank
7. A fleet
8. A prison
9. A convent
10. A station
11. A city
12. A team
13. An orchestra
14. A post office
15. A law court
16. The police

17. A political party

18. cA trade union

19. A navy

20. An army

B.   Give each idiomatic expression its right meaning from below:

1. To be in the same boat.

2. With flying colours.

3. A queer fish.

4. To beat about the bush.

5. By hook or by crook.

6. To prick up one's ears.

7. To keep a thing dark.

8. To turn a deaf ears.

9. In black and white.

10. A stone's throw.

11. To know the ropes

12. A storm in a teacup.

MEANING

Not to come to the point.

To keep something secret.

A good knowledge of things.

In a similar difficulty.

A short, petty quarrel.

A very odd character.

To have it in writing.

Very successfully.

By any possible means.

To pretend not to hear.

To listen very carefully.

A short distance only.

C. Copy these sentences below and say which one is:

1. A proverb
2. An advertisement
3. A riddle
4. A joke
5. A tongue twister
6. A recipe
7. An inscription
8. A receipt
9. A public notice

a) WANTED. Boy's second-hand bicycle for cash. Phone 084 4456 702

b) Presented to Kennedy Mkalipi for bravery. B. Dukada. Mayor.

c) What is so sad about a calendar?

d) A bird in the hand is worth two in the bush.

e) The mail ship was unable to leave. The harbour entrance was blocked by a sardine

f) Received with thanks the sum of R678. Signed: M. Bali.

g) WARNING: Trespassers will be prosecuted. By Order.

h) Peter Piper picked a peck of pickled peppers.

i) For pancakes: 110g flour, ½ teaspoon salt, 2 teaspoons baking powder, ¼ litre milk, 1 to 2 eggs. Beat up well.

D. Give each proverb its right meaning chosen from below:

1. It's no use crying over spilt milk.
2. A fool and his money are soon parted.
3. Look before you leap.
4. Don't count your chicken before they are checked.
5. Like father, like son.
6. Once bitten, twice shy.
7. The early bird catches the worm.
8. Too many cooks spoil the broth.

MEANINGS

a) Do not rush into things without thinking.

b) A child often resembles his parents.

c) The person who gets in first has the better chance.

d) A task is often badly done if too many people are in charge.

e) An unhappy experience makes one careful in future.

f) A stupid person spends money recklessly.

g) It is useless to worry over what cannot be remedied.

h) Do not rely on your plans until they have been fulfilled.

E. Use each of these verbs to complete the sentences below:

Waddled, galloped, wallowed, charged, trotted, strutted, scampered, frisked

a) The horse………past the winning post.
b) The pigs………in the deep mud.
c) A frightened mouse………across the room.
d) The ducks………down to the pond.
e) Two peacocks…….proudly across the lawn.
f) The bull……….into the huge arena.
g) Lambs……….playfully in the meadow.
h) The donkey………..slowly behind its master.

23.4. Punctuation

- **Punctuate correctly:**

Don't you think you'd better go now said the old dustbin to the mouse inside it certainly not answered the mouse I am enjoying myself its dangerous to stay any longer sighed the dustbin who cares for danger replied the mouse cockily there's someone coming be quick whispered the dustbin pah Sneered the mouse why worry suddenly the dustbin was lifted up and minutes later the mouse was sailing through the air amidst cabbage stalks empty tins broken cups peels bottles and slops straight into the municipal dirt lorry

23.4.5. Reading and Reasoning Activity

WHY MANNERS?

Almost all of us believe that we live in an age of uncouth manners, that things were better in sane previous era. For example, the eighteenth century in England is known as a period of high refinement in social intercourse. We look back with nostalgia to the soft candlelight, the elaborate courtesies, the hand kissing – unwilling to confront the brutal reality of a century in which duelling to the death was common place and gentlemen were expected to drink themselves under the table.

Manners change. In our day, it is considered good manners to be clean – indeed we spend millions on products designed to keep us "fresh". In the eighteenth century, by contrast, most doctors and church authorities frowned on bathing, and women's extravagant coiffures were often infested with lice.

The changeability of manners makes the whole subject difficult to approach. To take one example: it was not considered bad manners in the eighteenth century to wear your hat indoors. You would take it off to greet a lady, then put I back on. The reason for this is plain. The hat served as the badge of rank throughout most of history, a visible mark of status, in the second place, you couldn't draw a sword easily if you were holding a hat in your hand.

There is a lesson to be learnt from this. For the most part, manners are merely self-protective devices appropriate to the customs of a particular age. These customs sometimes become formalized and symbolic, but they are invariably derived from some practical need. Thus, on meeting somebody, we commonly shake right hands-a formal custom of no present day significance. But in an age when everybody carried weapons, it was a demonstration that one was prepared to converse without a weapons in one's hand, a sign of peace.

What we think of as good manners was merely a way of saying, "I mean you no immediate violence, if you can show that your intention is the same."

In a similar spirit, the seat on the right hand of the host is the place of honour. One theory about the origin of this custom is that a right handed man sitting in the host's right could not easily stab him. What had been the prudent place for a rival gradually became the honoured seat for any important guest.

Caution lies behind manners, wherever we look. In days gone by, a host sampled the wine before serving it, not to check that the wine steward used his polished wine server as demonstration of the host's good will towards his guests. Silver was thought to neutralize poisons in wine.

Why do we stand aside and let someone older or more important go through the door first? One theory is that in medieval times it was sensible for the strongest man to leave the castle first, since there was always a possibility he would be met with armed opponents or the rebellious peasantry waving pitchforks and scythes. Gradually a certain honour descended upon this position. It was assumed that the most important person was also the strongest, and even if he wasn't he could hardly deny it.

Manners are society's way of oiling the machinery. People with good manners do better in most situations are impossible without good manners, which explains why diplomats are formed for their courtesy. The best lawyers, too, are usually exquisitely courteous. Beware of the man who never raises his voice and always treats you with courtesy he could be going for the jugular.

In the nineteenth century, most of the great gunfighters of the American West were notorious for their florid good manners; being all too aware that if they let things get out of hand, they would have to draw and shoot. Good manners helped those men survive, since even the best gunfighter could win only so many gunfights before his luck ran out. They were not "big-talking men", they were softly spoken and courteous. Despite mankind's reputation for violence, most people prefer to avoid confrontation, avoiding confrontation is what manners are all about. Manners represent the triumph of civilization over barbarism, and the sensible application of enlightened self-interest. Manners are not weaknesses but common-sense.

In the end, there is no gain in being cruel to people, whether it is in the small failures of civility in daily life or in the larger ones. Manners are mankind's way of saying, "Let's not fight unless we have to, and there is no higher wisdom than that, in diplomacy, in business, in love, in the transactions of everyday life.

Micheal Korda, Readers Digest, 1988

A. How Well Did You Read?

1. Why is the eighteenth-century England regarded as the period of high refinement in social intercourse?

2. Compare and contrast good manners in modem times with good manners in the eighteenth century.

3. Give two reasons why it was not considered bad manners in the eighteenth century to wear your hat indoors.

4. Explain briefly what is common between the custom of hand-shaking in the eighteenth century and nowadays.

5. Explain why the seat on the right hand of the host is the "place of honour".

6. How did the host show his guests the good will in the eighteenth century?

7. Why do we stand aside and let someone older or more important go through the door first?

8. In your own words, briefly explain what good manners are.

B. How Many New Words Did You Learn?

1. How does a person of uncouth manners behave?

2. A period of high refinement in social intercourse relates to….of the society.

3. Nostalgia refers to………of the past.

4. A duel is………by two men with.

5. What sort of gentlemen drink themselves under the table?

6. Most doctors arid church authorities frowned on bathing, that means, they (approved, disapproved, encouraged) cleanliness.

7. Women's extravagant coiffures refers to costly………

8. The prudent place is a……..place.

9. Wine was sampled by…….it before the host served the wine to his guest.

10. Give an example of the year in medieval times.

11. Is it true or false: Peasantry are rebels. Substantiate your answer.

12. What is courtesy?

13. To go for the jugular mean to………

14. A notorious man is well-known for…………

15. To let Things get out of hand means to…………..

16. Give a typical example of triumph of civilization over barbarism.

Unit 12
Parts Of Speech

24. Gerund and Phrasal Noun

24.1. GERUND

24.1.1. A gerund is formed by adding -ing to the infinitive form of the verb. It is therefore a verbal noun:

- Reading improves knowledge. (Subject of "improves")
- He likes reading. (Object of "likes")
- He is fond of helping the needy. (Object of preposition "of")

24.1.2. General rules in the correct use of a gerund:

- The following verbs are followed by a gerund and not by an infinitive
    1. Avoid arguing over petty things.
    2. Detest walking late
    3. Dislike going………
    4. Mind helping………
    5. Suggest asking her………

6. Consider going………

7. Deny having………

8. Finish working………

9. Risk losing it………

10.   Stop working………

- When a verb is followed by a preposition, a gerund is used and not an infinitive:

1. aim at passing………

2. insist on coming………

3. read without understanding………

4. apologize for disturbing………

5. look forward to going there.

6. refrain from doing it.

- Expressions that are followed by a gerund:

1. in danger of falling………

2. little point in trying………

3. no use bothering………

4. no purpose in waiting……

- Use of possessive case before a gerund:

1. He does not like your inviting them (Not-you)

2. He did not like Peter's coming so late (Not-Peter)

24.1.3. Complete these sentences by filling in the correct form of the verb in brackets:

a) Tell him (go) now.

b) I dislike (say) it.

c) He wants (sleep).

d) We could not help (laugh).

e) She enjoys (work) hard.

f) Aim at (persuade) him.

g) Did he object to your (help) him?

h) They decided (go).

i) There is little purpose in your (go).

j) Please excuse my (interrupt) you.

k) Do you remember (see) it?

l) Did he deny (tell) you?

m) His (resign) was considered the non-event by the Board of Directors.

n) (See) is believing.

o) It stopped (rain).

24.2. Phrasal Nouns

A phrasal noun is a compound noun made up of a verb + adverbial participle or adverbial participle + verb.

24.2.1. Find out from your dictionary the meanings of the following phrasal nouns and use each in a sentence:

1. breakaway

2. breakthrough
3. breakdown
4. break-up
5. break-in
6. changeover
7. clear-up
8. closedown
9. come-back
10. come-on
11. cut-down
12. get-together
13. give-away
14. go-between
15. handout
16. hangover
17. hold up
18. layout
19. leftover
20. let-down
21. line- up
22. look- in
23. make-up
24. payout
25. round-up
26. runaway

27. sell-out
28. sendoff
29. setback
30. set-up
31. showdown
32. standby
33. tie-up
34. turnover
35. walkout
36. walkover
37. warm-up
38. wash-out
39. by product
40. bystander

24.3. Improve Your Vocabulary

24.3.1. Use each of these phrases in a suitable sentence to show clearly its meaning:

a) To be at large.

b) To be in form.

c) To be on time.

d) To be in a bad way.

e) To be at a loose end.

f) To be worthwhile.

24.3.2. Replace each expression with one word. The clue is given in brackets.

(a) to come closer (ap)

(b) without hair (b)

(c) he steals (b)

(d) written on an envelope (ad)

(e) large branches (bo)

(f) a sea-trip (v)

(g) a place for books (l)

(h) used for boiling water (k)

(i) stoppered glass flask into which wine or spirit is poured off (d)

(j) dark outline of person or thing against lighter background (si)

24.3.3. Use each of the following words in suitable sentences that clearly show each word has two or more different meanings:

(1) post

(2) safe

(3) park

(4) boil

(5) hail

(6) fine

(7) tap

(8) ring

(9) ground

(10) hold

24.3.4. Fill in the correct collective nouns:

1. A……..of bread
2. A……..of boats
3. A……..of eggs
4. A……..of judges
5. A……..of whales
6. A……..of pearls
7. A……..of arrows
8. A……..of diamonds
9. A……..of policeman
10. A……..of stars

Collective Nouns

Galaxy, rope, batch, sheaf, posse, clutch, school, cluster, flotilla, bench

24.4. Punctuation

- Punctuate the following correctly:

when Alexander Graham was a young man the telegraph was invented by Mr Samuel Morse his Morse code soon became world famous this made it possible to transit messages in "dots" and "dashes" over the air by switching an electric current on and off with a button alexander bell however was determined to find a way of sending real spoken words along a wire he eventually invented the telephone

24.5. Reading and Reasoning Activity

WHAT MEN REALLY THINK ABOUT WOMEN

To start with, men actually like women. This should be obvious. But for more than a decade, men and women have both been subjected to an avalanche of humourless feminist rhetoric saying the opposite.

We were told that men essentially saw women as unpaid domestic labour, fit only to be treated as chattel. Sober lectures were delivered about male fixation on female anatomy to the exclusion of all other properties. Men were depicted as cruel oafs, lacking any sense of justice. The valuable part of all this sound and fury was fuelled by a serious demand for social equality.

Fortunately, all through that unhappy period, most men continued to like women. They loved them, broke up with them, and married them. They had children with them. They even made a valiant attempt to understand them.

Today, I think I know what men want from women. Here is the list of qualities men admire most in women.

1. Intelligence

Men are not interested in slow-witted or purposefully ignorant women. Men of all ages express contempt for the smart woman who plays dumb out of fear her intelligence will turn men off. They contend that if she hides her brains, she'll hide other things too.

Men make a clear distinction between ignorance and stupidity. Ignorance is a lack of knowledge, easily remedied by intelligent human beings. Most men have little interest in settling down with truly stupid women.

2. Humour

Men usually realise that laughter is the best remedy for the difficulties of living, and a sense of humour is highly prized. "I really love my wife," one friend of mine says, "because she makes me laugh."

"She cheers me up," another say about his mate.

3. Self-reliance

These days, men are much more attracted to the idea of woman as partners than as dependents. So they talk admiringly of women who have careers and their own sources of income. The self-reliant woman, confident in her own abilities to function, can cheer her man's work and isn't jealous of its burden on his time and energy.

Self-reliance isn't simply a matter of economics. Men make some of their most brutal jokes about the whimpering female who can't hail a taxi without male help. In spite of the changing roles of women, this helpless type persists. Some insecure men are still attracted to them. But to most men, they are just a pain.

4. Beauty

Although men are still strongly attracted to beautiful women, the standards of physical beauty are undergoing a gradual redefinition. Men express open admiration for women who are healthy, well-groomed and confident.

On the other hand, few men have patience with women who constantly discuss their diets or their health clubs. Health is one thing, narcissism quite another.

Adapted from the article, by Pete Hamill. Readers Digest, 1988.

A. How Well Did You Read the Passage?

1. Mention any three stereotypes that are regarded as humourless feminist rhetoric?

2. Explain the real human relationship between men and women.

3. What "other things" will a smart woman who plays dumb hide?

4. How is ignorance remedied by intelligent human beings?

5. Why do most men like women with sense of humour?

6. By self-reliance men like women who are……and……independent.

7. According to this survey, the beauty that men appreciate refers to the……. and…….women.

B. How Many New Words Did You Learn?

1. Find the clause that simply means the lie (Paragraph 1)

2. Give the opposite of "obvious" (para. 1)

3. Chattel means (servant, mere possession, slave)

4. Male fixation on female anatomy means males regard females…..as objects.

5. An oaf depicts a man without…….

6. A smart woman is an………woman.

7. What is the difference between ignorance and stupidity?

8. A highly prized thing is an…….thing.

9. What sort of a female is a whimpering female?

10. Find the word in tire last paragraph that refers to a person who is obsessed with self-admiration.

C. How Well Do You Know Your English Grammar?

1) Form adjectives from the following words

Actually, essentially, exclusion, equality, intelligence, contempt, fear, knowledge, laughter, cheers, time, energy

2) Form abstract nouns from the following words

Treated, valuable, serious, continued, contend, remedied, truly, really, friend, admiringly, attracted, insecure.

Unit 13
Direct and Indirect Speech

25.1. Direct Speech

Direct speech quotes the actual words used by the speaker, and the actual words are put within the invented commas:

"I feel drowsy," said Don.

"What did you say?" Penny asked.

"Go and sleep now!" ordered Don's mother.

25.2. Indirect or Reported Speech

Reported speech gives the words of the speaker as reported by someone else or by the speaker himself.

25.2.1. Here are the rules for changing Direct to Reported Speech:

A. **Removal of Inverted Commas**

B. **Tense Changes:**

- After a reporting verb in a present, present perfect or future tense the verb in the direct speech does not change:

Don says, "I feel drowsy."

Don says he feels drowsy.

"I have slept late," says Don.

Don says that the he has slept late.

Penny says, "I shall bring your supper."

Penny says that she shall bring his/her supper.

- After a reporting verb in a past tense, the verb in direct speech is changed into a past tense:

Don said, "I feel drowsy.

Don said that he felt drowsy.

"I have slept late," said Don.

Don said that he had slept late.

Penny said, "I shall bring your supper."

Penny said that she would bring his/her supper.

A past tense in the direct speech changes into the past perfect tense after a reporting verb in a past tense:

Don said, "I slept late."

Don said that he had slept late.

C. Pronouns

- When the dialogue is reported by a third person, pronouns of the first and second persons are usually changed into those of the third person

"I spoke about it to you," said Don to Penny.

Don told Penny that he had spoken about it to her.

- Similarly, I becomes she/he.

Me becomes him/her.

We becomes they, and

Us becomes them.

D. Other Pronouns

- The following pronouns change as follows after a past reporting verb

This changes to that.

There changes to those.

E. Adverbs of Time and Place

- The following adverbs stay the same after a present reporting verb:

Now, here, ago, tonight, this week, tomorrow, today:

She says, "I am drowsy now."

She says that she is drowsy now.

- After a past reporting verb the above adverbs undergo the following changes:

Now changes into then

Here changes into there

Ago changes into before/previously

Yesterday changes into the previous day

Tonight, changes into that night

This week changes into that week

Last night changes into previous night

Today changes into that day

Tomorrow changes into the next/the following day

F. Questions and Commands

- Direct questions are converted into statements and introductory words such as the following are used:

"Did you do your homework?"

She/he asked whether he/she had done his/her homework.

"Why did you not do your homework?"

The teacher enquired why he/she/they had not done his/her/their homework.

Note that no question mark appears at the end of the indirect speech form

- Direct Commands are changed into reported speech in two ways:

a) By the use of introductory words such as: told, ordered, or urged (for request) followed by should or ought:

"Bring your homework," the teacher told the students.

The teacher told the students that they should bring their homework.

b) The infinitive "to" is used instead of "should" or "ought":

The teacher told the students to bring homework.

G. Exclamations

Exclamations are best conveyed by reporting verbs embodying the mood of the original exclamation:

i. "What a lovely dress, this is!"

She remarked what a lovely dress that was.

ii. "Careful!"

He warned…

iii. "Yes!"

He agreed.

iv. "Bad luck!"

She expressed her sympathy…

v. "Help!" She called for help.

vi. "Ha ha!"

She laughed.

vii. "Excuse me!"

   She interrupted.

viii. "No!"

   He refused.

ix. "Please!"

   She begged.

x. "Hello!"

   She greeted her friend.

xi. "Good gracious me!"

   He was astonished.

25.2.2. Practising Activity

A.   Re-write in reported speech:

   a) "I shall go tomorrow, if I can", said Peter to John.

   b) "We expect to leave here tomorrow," said Tom.

   c) "I shall be ready in five minutes," said Rachel.

   d) "It is now too late to finish this week," said the teacher.

   e) "We would like to go tonight if it is possible," said Albert.

   f) "You should like to go now," said Peter to Fred.

   g) "I am sorry, there is nothing left, sir," said Tom.

   h) "I did see it but a long time ago," said Peter.

   i) "Poor me!" said the boy. "I have spent all my pocket money."

   j) "Here is the place where I found it," said Lucy.

B. Put the following sentences into reported speech with the reporting verb in the PAST TENSE. Vary the reporting verb: he asked, enquired, wondered, wanted to know, etc.

1. "Where are you going?"
2. "How did you do that?"
3. "Who will come to the cinema with me?"
4. "When will my dress be finished?"
5. "Why are you so sad?"
6. "What is the matter?"
7. "Which book are we taking?"
8. "Where ought we to meet tonight?"
9. "Who showed you my work?"
10. "How could you be so unkind?"
11. "When did they tell you that?"
12. "Why has she not eaten anything?"
13. "What am I to do?"
14. "What is the time?"
15. "How do you know that?"
16. "Where has he put my pencil?"
17. "When are you beginning your holiday?"
18. "Where can I go for it?"
19. "How do you like this cake?"
20. "Why does he sing so loudly?"

C. Put the following into reported speech with the reporting verb in the past tense:

1. "What a lovely house!"
2. "Hello! What do you want?"
3. "My goodness! You're slim!"
4. "What a dirty face you have!"
5. "Oh! I've cut myself!"
6. "Help me!"
7. "The house is no fire!"
8. "What have you done to your hair?"
9. "Good gracious! It's impossible!"
10. "What on earth has happened?"
11. "What a terrible noise!"
12. "Be quiet!"
13. "Don't stand there doing nothing!"
14. "What a fool I've been! Why didn't I think of it before?"
15. "What a noise you're making! Do you call that playing the piano?"
16. "What a pity we didn't eat up all the figs yesterday!
17. "I say, what a charming daughter you have. Mrs Nkosi!
18. "What a big helping of pudding you've given me!"
19. "Look-out! There's a truck coming."
20. "Hooray! We're going to have a holiday tomorrow!"

25.3. Phrasal Nouns

Use the phrasal nouns in short sentences that illustrate their meanings: e.g. We could not travel after the downpour, the road became slippery.

1. downpour
2. forebear
3. foresight
4. input
5. insight
6. offshoot
7. offspring
8. onlooker
9. outcome
10. output
11. oversight
12. overthrow
13. upkeep
14. uproar
15. uphold

25.4. Improve Your Vocabulary

A.   Match the idiomatic expressions in Column A with their meanings in Column B

Column A	Column B
(a) Up in arms.	Both sides yielding a little.
(b) Behind the scenes.	Fail to keep one's positions.
(c) Lose ground.	Ready to fight.
(d) Stand one's ground.	In secret, away from the public eye.
(e) Give and take.	Be very careful.
(f) Take pains.	Not to yield.

B. Write down one word for each of the following expression:

a) To leave out.

b) Shelf above a fireplace.

c) Make a liquid weaker by adding water.

d) Eagerly and seriously.

e) Place where two things join.

f) Piece of land almost surrounded by water.

g) Narrow channel of water joining two larger stretches of water.

h) Go on board a ship.

i) Something that is fit to be eaten.

j) Person who listens to the conversation of others, without their realizing it.

WORDS

Mantelpiece, earnestly, omit, dilute, edible, peninsula junction, strait, embark, eavesdropper.

C. Explain the meaning of each adjective in each pair of phrases:

1) A sharp knife.

A sharp boy.

2) A poor man.

A poor joke.

3) A hard wood.

A hard parent.

4) A deep cut.

A deep respect.

5) A bad boy.

A bad onion.

6) A wild bird.

A wild night.

D. In each sentence replace the underlined words with one word similar in meaning:

a) Father had some money put by for my education.

b) The match had to be put off a fortnight.

c) The clock was put forward one hour.

d) She told him to put on his new blazer.

e) The criminal was put away for ten years.

25.5. Punctuation activity for learners:

- Punctuate correctly :
- michael faraday was the son of a yorkshire blacksmith who moved to London michael spent twenty years experimenting to find out how to make electricity he succeeded in 1831 with apparatus consisting of a magnet a copper disc and wire he made or induced an electric current it was the beginning of the

dynamo or electric generator which produces electricity for power and light throughout the modem world

25.6. Reading and Reasoning

Some Famous People

1. Roald Amundsen, the Norwegian reached the South Pole in 1911, followed three weeks later by Robert E. Scott, the Englishman, who found there the Norwegian flag fluttering from two skis that Amundsen had planted in the ice.

2. Lord Robert Baden-Powell, the British, founded the Boy Scout Movement in 1908, which rapidly spread throughout the world.

3. Langelo Biro, the Hungarian, invented the ballpoint in 1938 after he had experienced the blotting of his work by ink.

4. Melville Bissel, the American of Chicago, invented the carpet sweeper after he was troubled time and again by dust problem in his shop.

5. "General" William Booth, the British, founded the Salvation Army in 1878. Today the Salvation Army has branches in every country in the whole world.

6. Madame Marie Curie, the French, who lived from 1867 to 1934, discovered together with her husband, Professor Pierrre Currie, the radium, the powerful substance used chiefly in the treatment of cancer.

7. Charles Goodyear, the American, discovered the art of vulcanizing rubber and thus founded the tyre industry.

8. Sir Edmund Hillary, the New Zealander became the first persons together with Scherpa Tenzing Norgay to reach in 1953 the world's highest mountain, Mt Everest.

9. William Richard Morris, Lord Nuffield, became the pioneer of the British motor industry in producing such popular makes of cars such as the Morris, Austin, Riley and Wolsely. He donated most of his immense fortune to medical research, hospitals, sport organizations and various charities.

10. Rear Admiral Edwin Peary, the America, reached the North Pole with his African American assistant, Matthew Henson, and four Eskimos on the 6 April 1909.

11. Louis Pasteur, the French, born in 1822 and died in 1894 was the brilliant chemist. He discovered that microscopic living germs or bacteria, were the cause of numerous diseases, and as a result he found many remarkable remedies.

12. Dr Albert Schweitzer, the German founded the hospital at Lamberene in the hot wet jungle of West Africa where he devoted his life to the care of African suffering from leprosy and other tropical; diseases

How Well Did You Read the Passage?

1. Of what significance was the discovery of Roald Amundsen to the humankind? What has been the contribution of Boy Scout Movement since 1908?

2. Before the invention of the ballpoint, what was used for writing?

3. Mention at least three brands of carpet sweepers which have been developed from Melville Bissel's invention.

4. How has the Salvation Army contributed to society since 1878?

5. Explain briefly how the radium is used in the treatment of cancer.

6. Briefly explain the art of vulcanizing rubber.

7. Of which mountain is the summit of Mt Everest?

8. Do you agree that Lord Nuffield is also a philanthropist? Substantiate your answer.

9. Who are the natives of the North Pole?

10. What is pasteurization?

11. What are the symptoms of leprosy?

B. How Many New Words Did You Learn?

1) Explain the meaning of the words:

- Explorer
- Inventor
- Discoverer
- Founder
- Pioneer

2) For what purpose is each of these instruments used?

- A barometer
- A gas meter
- A thermometer
- A speedometer

Unit 14
Active Voice and Passive Voice

26.1. Active Voice

- A verb is in the active voice when it tells us what the subject does:

  My brother helps me.

26.2.1. Passive Voice

- A verb is in the passive voice when it tells us what is done to the subject or what the subject experiences:

  I am helped by my brother.

26.2.2. Changes That Take Place When a Verb Is Changed from Active Voice to Passive Voice

a) The OBJECT of the verb in the active voice becomes the SUBJECT of the verb in the passive voice:

Subject	Verb	Object
My brother	Helps	Me (active voice)
I	Am helped	By my brother (passive voice)

b) Pronouns in the object form change to the subject form; vice versa

Subject Form	Object form
I	Me
He	Him
She	Her
We	Us
They	Them

c) The verb changes its form, but not its tense. Here are some of the main changes:

Active voice	Passive voice
Catches	Is caught
Is catching	Is being caught
Has caught	Has been caught
Caught	Was caught
Was catching	Was being caught
Had caught	Had been caught
Will catch	Will be caught
Will be catching	Will being caught
will have caught	Will have been caught
Can catch	Can be caught
Could catch	Could be caught
Might catch	Might be caught

d) The verb is followed by "by" and the original subject:

- The girl is catching the ball. (Active Voice)

- The ball is being caught by the girl. (Passive Voice)

e) Intransitive verbs (verbs that do not take an object) cannot be used in the Passive Voice: talk, flow, wait, come, seem, wander etc.

f) When a verb in the active voice has two objects, in the passive voice, it is preferable to make the PERSONAL OBJECT the subject of the passive voice:

- Active Voice: My wife gave me a present.
- Passive Voice: I was given a present by my wife.

g) The word "by" followed by the subject may be omitted when what has been done is more important than the person who did it:

- Active Voice: The policeman has just arrested the thief.
- Passive Voice: The thief has just been arrested.
- Active Voice: Someone has made a mistake.
- Passive Voice: A mistake has been made.

26.2.3. Practising Activity

A. Put the following sentences into the Passive Voice by beginning each sentence with the underlined words:

1. Themba helps Zola.
2. He helps him.
3. Themba and Zola helped the children.
4. They helped them.
5. Themba will help Zola.
6. He will help him.
7. I can help her.
8. They may help them.
9. He has helped us.
10. I have helped him.

11. They had helped her.

12. She is helping him.

13. He was helping them.

14. She will be helping me.

15. We will have helped her.

B.　Put the following sentences into the Passive Voice, and omit "by" where you think these words are unnecessary:

1. She showed the visitors the sitting room.

2. Someone asked the student a very difficult question.

3. We must look into this matter.

4. People speak well of my friend.

5. They told her to be quick.

6. Someone reads to the children every evening.

7. Somebody told me to wait outside.

8. Someone promised us bicycles if we passed our examinations.

9. You must work for success.

10. Somebody gave her a box of chocolates for her birthday.

11. I told them never to come here again.

12. They give him R10 change at shop.

13. She promised him a present on his birthday.

14. It is time they brought the cows in.

15. They told me to go away.

16. Nobody has slept in that room for years.

17. She will look after the little girl well.

18. A car ran over the dog.

19. The teacher promised us prizes if we worked well.

20. The friend told me the news this morning.

C.   Re-write this passage into the Passive Voice (Omit by)

The Experiment

Someone fastens firmly the metal bar into a piece of wood at one end of the base. Something supports it at the other end on a triangular block. Someone fixes a wooden rod into the base so that the metal bar rests against it.

Someone then heats the metal bar with a Bunsen burner. Someone moves with the flame along the whole length of the bar so that someone heats each part.

Observations:

As someone heats the bar, it expands. Although the expansion is small, someone can record and measure it on the scale.

26.3. Improve Your Vocabulary

26.3.1. What is the difference between a jungle, a forest, a wood, a plantation?

26.3.2. Use these words in suitable sentences:

1. fair, fare
2. grate, great
3. sale, sail
4. raise, rays
5. seams, seems

6. board, bored

7. rain, reign

8. ball, bowl

9. soot, suit

10. heir, hair

11. Stare, stair

12. Loan, lone

26.3.3. Replace the given word by word similar in meaning in accordance with the clues in brackets.

1. poetry (ve…)

2. miserable (wr…)

3. storehouse (wa…)

4. two weeks (fo…)

5. heaviness (we…)

6. dumb (mu…)

7. to give way (yi…)

8. to sparkle (gl…)

9. to grumble (co…)

10. to frown (sc…)

11. to copy (im…)

12. to annoy (ir…)

26.3.4. Explain the meaning of:

a) To keep watch.

b) Stabs of pain.

c) A gnawing ache.

d) A twitching tail.

e) Twin searchlights.

f) A slinking shape.

g) The brow of the hill.

h) The vicious brute.

i) Putting the final touches.

j) To have brains.

26.3.5. Replace each group of words with a word that begins with "m":

1. A lion has one.
2. One's best work.
3. Attracts steel objects.
4. Chop up finely.
5. Damp or wet.
6. Afternoon performance a cinema.
7. A large house.
8. A wooden hammer.
9. A feeding trough.
10. One who builds with stones.

26.3.6. Explain the meaning of the underlined idiomatic expressions:

a) I have a bone to pick with you about your remark.

b) As he entered, my heart was in my mouth.

c) The distance is 300 kilometres as the crow flies.

d) The coward showed a clean pair of heels.

e) Zandi looked daggers at the impudent man.

f) Grandpa Paul has become very hard of hearing.

g) Zola made no bones about asking him his business.

h) In the squabble between the children Mavis simply sat on the fence.

i) Now that Hillary is engaged, she is walking on air.

j) Thembi is the apple of her father's eye.

26.3.7. Pair off the proverbs in Column A with their meanings in Column B, and then write sentences that illustrate the meanings of the proverbs:

Column A	Column B
(a) Necessity is the mother of invention	It is important to win he final battle early set-backs are less important
(b) He who laughs the best laughs the last.	Important happenings are usually preceded by warnings.
(c) Brevity is the soul of wit.	When you really need something you are then more likely to find remedy.
(d) Coming events cast their shadows before.	We do not feel the same respect for those whom we know well.
(e) Familiarity breeds contempt	There is no need to advertise goods of excellent quality.
(f) Take no thought for the marrow.	It does not cost much to speak well of others.

(g) Goods words are worth much and cost little.	Do not think about the future.
(h) Good wine need to bush	If you wish to be witty, you should say what you sat in as few words as possible.

26.3.8. Pair the adjectives with the corresponding nouns, and then use the pairs in sentences that illustrate their meanings :

ADJECTIVES

Embarrassing, spontaneous, preliminary, callous, impartial, authentic, vehement, adjacent, durable, religious, northern.

NOUNS

Reply, hemisphere, question, enquiries, material, room, beliefs, accounts, judge, behaviour, denial.

26.4. Punctuation

- **Punctuate Correctly**

    Keith Benson sat beneath a gaily coloured beach umbrella outside a cafe he was about to order a cool drink when a man slipped into the seat opposite I hope you don't object said the dark eyed stranger permit me to introduce myself he went on my name is Paul Reeves have you ever heard of me im afraid not replied Keith.

26.5. Reading and Reasoning Activity

Lessons at the Halfway Point

I am 40 years old: at halfway point. When my mind fixed on this, I felt a sense of panic. After a few weeks I settled down, making peace with the fact that we are, in the words of poet Carl Sandburg, "riding on a limited express". And then, by serendipity, I read an old Scout Manual about what to do when you are lost: Stop. Investigate. Go over everything you know. Continue forward if you are certain of your route. If you move, leave a note.

This is my note. The day I finished writing these lessons, I walked outside. Passing my neighbour I shouted, "How're you doing?"

His reply. "Best day yet!"

I decided to stand straighter. Posture like attitude, is important.

So here are my lessons, which I hope will comfort the afflicted while afflicting the comfortable.

1. Nothing is as stressful as trying to be a different person from whom you are.

2. When you stop spending time with real friends, you lose your balance.

3. Amazingly, people think the things that happen to them happen only to them.

4. The lies we tell ourselves are more pernicious than the lies we tell others: "I'm nothing like my mother", "I'm too busy to exercise", "I don't want to get married."

5. Those who are tentative about making plans are often unsure of their ability to arrive.

6. If you don't personally get to know people from other racial, religious or cultural groups, it's very easy to believe ugly things about them and make them frightening in your mind.

7. The majority of overweight people I know skip breakfast, and the majority of thin people don't. Some men spend more time maintaining their lawn than they do their relationship.

8. The most absolute dictator's power is not as great as a typical parent's power over a child.

9. I still place emphasis on appearance, even though I've run across a few well-

dressed idiots.

10. When you make a mistake, write down what you've learnt before a week passed. The process of writing it and reading it can help you avoid repeating it.

11. Three things that children must know who's the boss, what the rules are, and who's going to enforce them.

12. Some days for no perceptible reason, I feel scared, lonely and hopeless. After a good night's sleep or a talk to someone who holds my hand and tells me to keep going. I'm usually just fine.

13. I believe that people who work 12 hours a day should go home with bigger loaves of bread than people who work eight.

14. Some ideas are so stupid that only intellectuals could believe them.

15. Decide early in any situation exactly what your bottom line is, then stick to it.

16. Far more often than poverty breeds crime, crime breeds poverty.

17. If you don't defend your honour, people will assume you have none.

18. People who don't work are often more exhausted than people who do.

19. It is vital to give yourself credit for agony you have survived throughout life.

20. As you look at history, it's apparent that human behaviour is much easier to predict than the weather.

By Michael Levine. Reader's Digest. 1997

A. How Well Did You Read the Passage?

1. Literally, to what does the phrase "at the halfway point" refer?

2. In the context of human life, explain "if you move, leave a note."

3. The author's lessons are for the afflicted and the comfortable. Select any two lessons that are meant for the afflicted and explain how are such lessons

suitable for the afflicted. Second, choose any two lessons that relate to the comfortable, and explain in what way such lessons are suitable for the comfortable.

4. Explain what you think makes the most people who skip breakfast overnight in comparison to those thin people who do not skip breakfast.

5. Quote a proverb that summarises lesson number 9.

6. In your own words, briefly explain what the 13th lesson means.

7. With reference to lesson number 14, state one stupid idea that only intellectuals could believe.

8. Lesson number 14 is an irony. Explain its literal meaning.

9. According to the 16th lesson, how does crime breed poverty?

10. By means of an example, explain the gist of lesson number 20.

B. How Many New Words Did You Learn?

1. What does Carl Sandburg imply about life when he says we are "riding on a limited express"? (Para 1)

2. Find the word in paragraph which means to make happy discoveries by accident.

3. When a person loses his balance he…(lesson 2)

4. A pernicious lie is a…lie. (lesson 4)

5. What is the opposite of tentative? (lesson 5)

6. Something is perceptible if you can, or with one of your senses.

7. What is the synonym of "exhausted"? (lesson 18)

8. What is vital for a person before he reaches the halfway point?

9. Give an example of an agony as regards life. (lesson 19)

10. In the context of lesson 20 credit means _____ to yourself.

C. How Well Do You Understand Your Grammar?

1. Form the following parts of speech from these words:

Word	Verb	Noun	Adjective	Adverb
(1) Peace	(2)	(3)	(4)	(6)
(7) Note	(8)	(9)	(10)	
(11) Power	(12)	(13)	(14)	(15)
(16) Emphasis	(17)	(18)	(19)	(20)

Unit 15
BUILDING OF WORDS

- A useful way of forming new words is to add a prefix or a suffix to an existing word.

27. 1. Prefixes

- A prefix is a syllable or syllables placed in front of a word with the object of adding to or changing its meaning. Here are some examples of useful prefixes.

Prefix	Meaning	Examples
a-, ab-,	Away from	Avert, abnormal
Ad-	To	Adjoin
Al-	All	Always, altogether
Ambi-, amphi-	Both	Ambidextrous, amphibious
Ante-	Before	Antecedent
Nati-	Against	Antidote, antiseptic
Arch	Leader, chief	Archbishop
Archae-	Ancient	Archaeology, archaic
Anto-	Self	Autobiography
Bene-	well	Beneficiary
Bi-, bis-	Two/twice	Bilingual, bisect
Cata-, cath-	Down/throughout	Catapult, catholic
Circum-	Round	Circumference
Cis-	On this side	Ciskei

Co-, cel-, com-, con-, cor-	With/together	Co-operate, collaborate, combine, connect, corroborate
Contra-, counter-	Against	Contradict, counteract
De-	Down/away from	Descend, detract
Deca-	Ten	December, Decalogue
Demi-	Half	Demigod
Dia-	Through	Diagonal
Dis-	In two/apart/asunder	Dissyllable, dispel, dissect
Dys-	Ill/bad/difficult	Dysentery, dyslexia, dyspepsia
Epi	Upon	Epitaph
Equi-	Equal	Equivalent, equidistant
Eu-	Well	Eulogy, euphony
E, ex-	Out of, from	Emerge, exterior, exodus
Ex-	Former	Ex-President, ex-teacher
Extra-	beyond	Extraordinary
Fore-	Before	Forehead, foretell
Hemi-	Half	Hemisphere
Hepta-	Seven	Heptagon
Hetero-	Different	Heterogeneous
Hexa-	Six	Hexagon
Homo-	The same	Homogeneous
Hyper-	Beyond/above	Hyperbole
Inter-	Between	Intermediate, intervene
Juxta-	Near to	Juxtaposition
Meta-	Change	Metamorphosis
Mis-	Wrong	Mislead
Mono-	Alone/one	Monologue, monarch
Non-, ne-	Not	Nonsense, negate
o-, ob-, oc-, of-	Against/in the	Omit, obstacle, occasion
Op	Way of	Offend, oppose
Omni	All/universal	Omnipotent, omnivorous
Para-, par	Beside	Parallel, parable
Pene-	Almost	Peninsula

Penta-	Five	Pentagon
Per-	Through/thoroughly	Percolate, perfect
peri	around	Perimeter
Poly-	Many	Polygamy, polygon
Post-	After	Postscript, post-mortem
Pre-	Before	Preamble, precede
Pro-	Before	Prologue, prognosis
Pseudo-	False Apparent Supposed But not real	Pseudonym
Re-	Back/again	Rejoin, react, remit
Retro-	Backwards	Retrospect
Se-	Aside Apart	Seclude, separate
Semi-	Half	Semicolon, semicircle
Sub-	Under	
Almost	Submerge, submarine	
Super-	Above Over	Supernatural
Trans-	Across	Transplant, Transvaal
Tri-	Three	
Thrice	Triangle, triple, tripod	
Ultra-	Beyond	Ultra-violet
vice	In place of for	Vice chairman, viceroy

27.1.1. Prefixes that express opposites (antonyms)

1) Dis- disobey, dishonest, dislike etc.

2) In- insufficient, indirect

- When the first letter begins with m or p, l, r, or g, the following prefixes are used instead of in-.

im immortal, immovable, impossible

il illegal, illogical, illiterate etc.

ir irregular, irreplaceable, irreconcilable

ig ignoble

Note well

Dis- and in- do not always express opposites.

Dis- may also mean "apart or away",

While "in" may also mean "in or "within":

Disarm-…….to take away weapons

Disinfect to take away or destroy infection.

Ingrow……..to grow in

Inland……….in the interior of a country

3) N- None, Nor, Never

4) Non- Non-stop, non-member etc.

5) Un- uncertain, unforgettable, unscrupulous

27.1.2. Practising Activity

A. Using your dictionary where necessary write down two words that begin with:

1. ambi-
2. ante-
3. bene-
4. co-
5. de-
6. equi-
7. ex-
8. fore-

9. inter-

10. pre-

B. From the words you have formed, write short sentences that illustrate the use of the words you have chosen.

C. By adding prefixes to these words, form words that have an opposite meaning:

Moderate, secure, pleasant, either, perfect, experienced, smoker, resident, Believe, material, comfortable, tidy, mobile, accurate, religious, legitimate, written, reasonable, friendly

27.2. Forming of Verbs

Both prefixes and suffixes may be used to form verbs from other parts of speech, including other verbs:

Prefixes

Prefix	Examples
Be-	Befriend
Em-	Empower
En-	Endanger
Im-	Imprison

Suffixes

Suffix	Examples
-ate	Substantiate (Substance)
-e	Bathe (Bath)

-en	Quicken (quick)
-fy, ify	Simplify (Simple)
-ise, -ize	Advise (advice)
-ish	Civilize
-ie	Flourish (flower)
-ve	Handle (hand)
	Believe

27.2.1. Practising Activity

A. Form verbs from prefixes or suffixes:

Sweet, strength, advice, glory, crumb, thick, short, able, bitter, false, height, equal, sympathy, courage.

B. Form a verb from the underlined words

   1) to fat a pig.

   2) to grief over.

   3) to frost meat.

   4) to friend a lad.

   5) to joy a film.

   6) to cold off.

   7) to full a cup.

   8) to cloth a baby.

   9) to grass cattle.

   10) to shelf a plan.

   11) to success in.

   12) to gold frames.

   13) to knee down.

14) to courage thrift.

15) to bright a room.

27.3. Passive Voice

Begin the following sentences with the underlined words. Omit active subjects such as I, we, you, they, one, someone, nobody, people, a man, a boy, the servant, etc. Because they are very seldom worth mention in the passive construction.

1) Unkind remarks easily upset Nancy.

2) Somebody must finish the work.

3) Nobody can repair this broken vase.

4) What ought we to do about this?

5) What questions did the examiner set?

6) People play football all over the world.

7) Nobody has made any mistakes.

8) Hugh Masekela composed this piece.

9) A guide pointed out the Pyramids to me.

10) Somebody has left the gate open, and so the horses have run away.

11) Somebody must do something for these poor men.

12) She fell into the water because somebody pushed her.

13) People will simply laugh at you for your trouble.

14) They carried her into the house.

15) They showed me a beautiful painting.

16) Nobody has answered my question properly.

17) They left the wounded behind.

18) Somebody had brought this child up very badly.

19) They didn't tell me the truth about the situation.

20) They asked Daisy why she went about with a silly person like me!

27.4. Improve Your Vocabulary

A. Use these expressions in sentences that illustrate their meanings:

1) gain ground.

2) make game of.

3) as a general rule.

4) a hard and fast rule.

5) as a matter of fact.

6) give and take.

7) go to pieces.

8) safe and sound.

9) look down upon.

10) as is.

B. Complete these proverbs:

1) Experience is the best…

2) There is no royal road…

3) Two wrongs do not make…

4) One is never too old to…

5) A bad excuse is better…

6) Courtesy costs…

7) More haste, less…

8) Once a thief, always…

C. List A contains synonyms of words in List B and antonyms of words in List C Arrange the words in List B and C in their correct order

A	B	C
Keep	Stubborn	Clumsy
Skilful	Calamity	Arrogance
Prevent	Hold	Success
Stormy	Clever	Abandon
Expensive	Hinder	Reasonable
Obstinate	Clear	Severe
Mild	Keen	Calm
Sharp	Gentle	Compassionate
Misfortune	Pitiless	Allow
Ruthless	Shyness	Cheap
Bashfulness	Tempestuous	Blunt

Example

| Bashfulness | Shyness | Arrogance |

D. Write short sentences that illustrate the meanings of the words in List B

E. Explain briefly the meaning of:

1) Kindly regard

2) Moaned loudly

3) A droll appearance

4) Pitied her

5) Dried her eyes

6) An unguarded moment

7) To knock on the head

8) To be rescued

9) To turn out

10) Restrain their smiles

27.4. Punctuation

- Punctuate the following paragraphs: On Wednesday five excited children and a tall man stood watching the mail ship enter the harbour it was the last week of the June holiday at Durban Michael Jimmy and Joan had invited their friends Brian and Anne to stay with them

27.5. Reading and Reasoning

Tap Your Hidden Energy

1) Remember when you could barely keep your eyes open in class, yet were totally alert during hours of after-school sports practise? And how about that rush of energy at the beginning of a love affair, or during a challenging job situation, or at the approach of danger?

2) To the contrary we often feel drained, unable to drag ourselves to the simplest task. We leave those letters unanswered, that leaky tap unrepaired, and squander our best energy on menial tasks or in front of the babbling bath of television. Why?

3) A human being is the kind of machine that wears out from lack of use. We learn in high-school science that kinetic energy is associated with motion. The same is true of human energy: it comes into existence through use. You can't hoard it. As Frederick Pres often said, "I don't want to be saved, I want to be spent."

We possess enormous stores of potential energy, more than we could ever hope to use. If we could tap as little as an added ten per cent of this vast resource, our lives would be significantly altered.

4) Here's how to get started:

1) Get – and stay – in shape.

Physical fitness contributes enormously to energy in every respect of our lives. Often the best remedy for weariness is 30 minutes of aerobic exercise. Those people who feel good about their own bodies are more likely to use their energy for the good of others, than those who live sedentary, unhealthy lives.

2) Utilize anger

Everyone experiences anger. But we suppress the emotion so effectively that we forfeit the vigour that goes with it.

There are times when it's appropriate to get angry and let the world know it. But there's also the possibility of taking the fervid energy of indignation, even of rage, and putting it to work for positive purposes. When you feel your anger rising, choose to go to work furiously on a favourite project.

3) Accentuate the positive

Numerous studies suggest that people with a positive outlook on life suffer far less sickness than do those who see the world in negative terms. They also have more energy.

Tom Peters and Robert Waterman speak of "an almost spooky similarity of language" among managers of the country's most successful companies. They all stress value of positive attitude and the effectiveness of praise and other similar forms of positive feedback.

"The most successful managers," Peters told me, "are unwilling to tolerate the negative stuff." Peters cites one executive's opinion that very successful people had had "an obnoxiously high level of praise piled on them in childhood – praise to the point of embarrassment.

Even serious blows in life can give you extra energy by knocking you off dead centre, shaking you out of your lethargy, but not if you deny that the blows are real. Acknowledging the negative doesn't mean snivelling, it means facing the truth and then moving on.

Simply describing what's wrong with your life to a good friend is likely to make you feel better and energetic. Once you've dealt with the negative, you are free to concentrate on the best in yourself.

4) Tell the truth

"There's nothing more energizing to a corporation than for people to start telling one another the truth," says Will Schutz, a corporate consultant. Truth-telling works best when it involves revealing your own feelings, not when used to insult others and get your own way. It has a lot going for it – risk, challenge, excitement and most important, the release of all that energy.

5) Set priorities

In making any choice, you face a monstrous fact: to move in one direction you must forgo all others. To choose one goal is to forsake a very large number of other possible goals. A friend of mine, 30 years old and still looking for a purpose in life, said, "Our generation has been brought on the idea of keeping your option open. But if you keep all your options open, you can't do anything. "Indecision leads to inaction, which leads to low energy, depression, and despair."

Mental and spiritual lassitude is often cured by the clear intention to act. You can't do everything, but you can do one thing, and then another and another. It's better to make a wrong choice than none at all.

Begin by listing your priorities – for the day, for the week, for the month. Divide them into A, B and C categories. At the least, accomplish the A items. Try the same with long-term goals. Priorities do shift, and you can change them at any time. But simply getting them down in black and white adds clarity to your life, and clarity creates energy.

6) Making commitments

There's nothing quite so energizing as a tough, firm deadline – as is well known to anyone who has faced an opening night curtain, a business deal closing date or a thesis due date.

The gift of an externally imposed deadline isn't always available and you might have to set one for yourself. But take it seriously. One way to do this is to make it public. Tell people who are important in your life. The firmer the deadline, the harder it is to break, the more energy it confers.

7) Keep on moving:

Don't go off half-cocked. Take time for wise planning. But don't take forever. Whatever you can do, or think you can do – begin it.

Always keep in mind that you can't hoard energy, you can't build it up by not using it. Adequate rest is part of any action plan, but unaccompanied by positive action, rest may only depress you.

It might well be that much depression and discontent can ultimately be traced to our unused energy, our untapped potential. There's enough constructive, creative work for everybody with plenty left over. All of us can increase our energy, starting now.

By George Leonard. Reader's Digest. 1988

A. How Well Did You Read The Passage

1) Give two examples that illustrate untapped hidden energy by persons.

2) Draw the difference between a human being as the kind of machine and an engine as the kind of machine.

3) Why is human energy analogous to kinetic energy?

4) Explain what Frederick Peris meant when he often said, "I don't want to be saved, I want to be spent."

5) Briefly explain how a person can increase his energy in order to accomplish constructive and creative work.

6) How does a positive outlook on life help a person?

7) What is the impact of "obnoxiously high levels of praise" that was given to a person in his childhood?

8) Explain the effects of truth-telling.

9) Give a practical example that illustrate the meaning of: "To choose one goal is to forsake a very large number of other possible goals."

10) State the effects of indecision.

11) Why does one have to tell people who are important to ones commitment in order to make a deadline firmer?

12) What is the significance of the firmer and harder deadline?

B.   How Many New Words Did You Learn?

1) To feel drained means to feel…(para. 2)

2) In the context of paragraph 2, menial tasks refer to (big, small) tasks.

3) What is the opposite of hoarding energy? (para 3)

4) Give the synonym of enormous (para 3)

5) A sedentary lifestyle is characterised by……….

6) Is it true? Vigour is another word for anger. Explain your answer. (para 5)

7) What is the difference between indignation and rage?

8) Replace this clause with one word:

a) People with a positive outlook on life.

b) People who see the world in negative terms.

9) Find the word in paragraph 8 which means "mentions".

10) "obnoxiously" means (offensively, insultingly, exaggeratedly) (para 8)

11) Priorities simply means first things……,………. things last, (para 12)

12) In one word, keeping your options open means. (para 12)

13) Lassitude means lack of………? (para 13)

14) To go off half-cocked means to………? (para 17)

15) In one word, "to take forever" to implement a plan means? (Para 17)

Unit 16
Forming of Nouns

- Nouns may be formed from other parts of speech by the use of suffixes, a suffix being a syllable or being syllables placed at the end of a word to form a new word or to change the meaning of a word

Here are some examples of the use of the suffixes in the forming of the nouns denoting persons and abstract nouns:

Suffix	Examples
-age	Breakage, passage
-al	Arrival, refusal
-ance	Avoidance, repentance
-ant	Inhabitant, dependant
-ar	Liar, scholar
-ary	Missionary, secretary
-action	Foundation, formation
-eer	Volunteer, auctioneer
-ence	Dependence, existence
-ent	Correspondent, superintendent
-er	Farmer, teacher
-(e) (ry)	Bravery, trickery
-hood	Childhood, neighbourhood
-ian	Brazilian, politician
-ee	Employee, interviewee
-ier	Cashier, clothier
-ing	Feeling, thinking
-ion	Collection, instruction
-ist	Tourist, typist
-ity	Absurdity, popularity

-man	Policeman, foreman
-ment	Development, government
-ness	Kindness, happiness
-or	Horror, accelerator
-or	Actor, professor
-ship	Friendship, membership
-ty	Cruelty, fifty
-y	Eighty, difficulty

28.1. Practising Activity

A. With the help of suffixes, form nouns denoting persons from these words, and then write a short sentence that illustrate the meaning of ten nouns that you have formed.

- Oppose, Egypt, serve
- Work, sail, assist
- Beg, fire, cycle
- Italy, sing, confide
- Swim, inhabit, burgle
- Lecture, watch, piano
- Desert, employ, engine
- Finance, sale, treasure

B. Form abstract nouns from these words by using suffixes other than -ing. Then use at least ten of the abstract nouns in short sentences that illustrate their meaning.

- Adopt, happy, obey,
- Permanent, endure, wise,
- Stupid, tempt, inform,

- Important, excel, humid,
- Meek, mock, humble,
- Brave, distinct, tender,
- Bold, active, multiply,
- Frequent, remove, partner,

28.2. Improve Your Vocabulary

A. Write down one word for each of these expressions:

a) Put off until a later date.

b) Cups, saucers and plates.

c) Strong desire to be or to do something.

d) Person who lives in a place.

e) Instrument for measuring the pressure of air.

f) Collection of wild animals in cages, particularly for use by a traveling show.

g) From now on.

h) Bring in goods from another country.

i) Person to whom money is owed.

j) Person who helps the enemies of his country

WORDS

- Crockery, traitor,
- Barometer, postpone,
- Menagerie, inhabitant,

- Henceforward, import,
- Creditor, ambition,

B. State very clearly what you think is the difference between:

a) a pin and a needle.

b) a glass and a jug.

c) a sock and a stocking.

d) a car and a cab.

e) scissors and shears.

C. From each of the following lines choose one word which is unlike others:

a) Lorry, train, bus, yacht, van, car.

b) Ascend, climb, mount, descend, rise.

c) Lawyer, judge, criminal, jury, theft.

d) Jump, hop, write, vault, skip.

e) Wheat, flower, oats, barley, rye, rice.

D. Choose the correct word from those in brackets:

a) A proposal is (an engagement, an idea, a suggestion).

b) (Bare, nude, clothed) is the opposite of naked.

c) Another word for regret is (pity, sorrow, envy).

d) A (cure, pill, drug) means the same as a remedy.

e) Pasture is land for growing (wheat, grass, fruit).

E. Show in sentences the two different meanings of each word:

Rings	Dates	Ports	Leaves
Arms	Bats	Scales	Ducks

Banks	Pains	Soles	Boils
Pests	Quarters	Ticks	Races

F. Give each proverb its right meaning:

a) A stitch in time saves nine.

b) Half a loaf is better than no bread.

c) Waste not, want not.

d) Better late than never.

e) Two heads are better than none.

f) One good turn deserves another.

g) Honesty is the best policy.

h) Slow and steady wins the race.

i) It never rains but it pours.

j) Fine feathers make fine birds.

Meanings:

- It is better to do a thing late than not at all.
- Always help those who have done you a good service.
- Smart clothes are no true test of a person's character.
- Pleasant or unpleasant things never come singly.
- To have a little of something is better than nothing.
- It often pays to seek the advice or opinion of someone else.
- Success may be achieved by steady though slow effort.
- Much time is saved by repairing thing immediately.

- The best rule in life is to be always honest.
- Practice thrift and the future will be safe.

28.3. Punctuation

Insert the Correct Punctuation:

Have you ever seen Olives John asked his mother yes at the grocers shop replied John don't you remember that I thought they're plums in the bottle oh yes said his mother they are like small plums

28.4. Reading and Reasoning Activity

Smoking's Fatal Excuses

1. My uncle smoked 20 cigarettes a day and lived to be 75.

2. Almost everyone knows a friend or relative in this category. However, the National Council Against Smoking estimates that half of all people who smoke throughout their adult years will be killed prematurely by their addiction, on average eight years early. Cigarettes will be responsible for the death of up to three million of the South African teenagers who smoke today if they continue their habit.

   Of the smokers over 65 who are still alive, many are disabled by bronchitis, angina, heart failure, or have had legs amputated. Only a small proportion survive in reasonable health to the age of 75 or more.

3. My aunt died of cancer yet she never smoked in her life.

   Not all cancers are caused by smoking. It is estimated by the WHO that one in three deaths from cancer can be attributed to tobacco. However, lung cancer, which accounts for more than 40 per cent of all male cancer deaths, is very uncommon in non-smokers. In a study of 401 newly diagnosed lung cancer patients at Cape Town's Groote Schuur Hospital in 1989, only 20 were non-smokers. Other cancers that are more common in smokers include those affecting the tongue, larynx, pancreas, bladder and cervix.

4. If someone dies of lung cancer you can't prove that it is because he/she smoked.

   Until last year, the link between lung cancer and smoking was based on statistical studies, and statistics do not provide proof concerning an individual Case. The change come after researchers at the City of Hope, a cancer research and treatment centre in California, analysed damage to the tumour – suppressor gene in human lung tissue by a chemical called BPDE, which is found in cigarette smoke.

   They found that BPDE is directly involved in the transformation of normal lung cells into cancer cells. The gene damage caused by BPDE matches exactly with several mutational: hot-spots specific to lung cancer, indicating that lung tissue is systematically damaged by the chemical.

5. People who don't smoke still suffer heart attacks.

   The narrowing and blockage of the coronary arteries, which causes angina and heart attacks, is due to a "fuming up" process in which the "fur" is the deposits of fat. This occurs in almost all of us as we get older, but it happens more in people with high blood pressure, diabetes, high blood-fat levels and in smokers.

   A British study of patients considered for coronary artery by-pass surgery for angina showed that 91% were smokers. Professor Ulrich Von Oppel, head of the cardiac thoracic unit at Groote Schuur Hospital estimates that 95–98 % of all bypass patients are smokers or ex-smokers.

6. The air pollution from motorcars and industry probably causes a lot of lung cancer.

   Lung cancer is more common in urban than in rural areas, because urban dwellers are generally more likely to smoke than their rural counterparts.

   Lung cancer is three times more common in men than in women. If air pollution rather than smoking were a prime cause, the lung-cancer rates should be much the same in both sexes.

   The British island of Jersey, which has few industrial femes and lots of fresh air, has had one of the world's highest rates of lung cancer. Cigarettes there are very cheap.

7. If I developed a serious illness such as heart disease, I'd give up.

   Unfortunately, the first sign of heart trouble for many people is a heart attack. Twenty five per cent of South Africans do not survive their first attack. Around 90% of people who develop it die within five years.

8. Low-tar cigarettes are safer.

   Smokers of low-tar cigarettes are slightly less liable to develop lung cancer than smokers of high-tar or non-filter cigarettes. But some filter deliver more carbon monoxide than the high-tar ones. So filter cigarettes cannot be considered safer for the heart and arteries.

9. If I give up I'll put on weight.

   This does not happen quite often but weight gain is controllable and the average weight gain after giving up smoking is only two kilograms. The health hazards of gaining weight are less than those of smoking.

10. A lot of people would be out of a job if everybody stopped smoking.

    There are about 5,300 South Africans employed solely in cigarette manufacture, and 25,000 more on tobacco farms. Several thousands more are involved in the packaging and selling of cigarettes. Currently about R7 billion is spent on cigarettes annually.

    If everyone stopped smoking, there would be job losses in the tobacco industry. However, the money these ex-smokers save on cigarettes would be spent elsewhere, thus creating jobs in other industries. In a household where both parents smoke a pack of 20 cigarettes a day, there would be more than R3,900 each year to spend on other things.

11. Pipes and cigars are safer.

    People who smoke pipers or cigars throughout their adult lives have only a slightly increased risk of premature death. However, cigarettes smokers who change to pipes or cigars still carry a substantial risk of lung cancer and bronchitis, probably because many continue to inhale the smoke.

12. Smoking doesn't cause any real harm to other people.

    Other people's smoke causes irritation to the nose and eyes. Some people with asthma or angina find their condition is aggravated by smoke. Evidence suggests that the non-smoking spouses of smokers have an increased incidence of lung cancer and heart disease. Similar considerations may apply to those exposed to tobacco smoke at work.

Heavy smoking in pregnancy increases the likelihood of the baby's dying before or after birth, and underweight babies are more common. The children of smoking parents are more likely to require hospital treatment for chest infections.

13. I've been smoking for 30 years – it's too late to give up.

The risk of a fatal heart attack in someone with no history of heart disease drops quite quickly with giving up smoking, within a few years the risks are not much greater than for a lifelong non-smoker. The 75% of patients who survive their first heart attack could halve the risk of a further heart attack if they never smoke again. It is a more effective measure than any drugs currently available.

The risk of developing lung cancer takes much longer to reduce, but ten to 15 years after stopping smoking, it is only slightly higher than for the non-smoker.

About a million South Africans are now ex-smokers. Thousands of them will be spared death from lung cancer and the rest have greatly improved their chances of living longer, healthier lives. So the sooner you stop smoking the better.

By Dr Barrie Smith.

For free professional advice about giving up smoking, call the tobacco or Health Information Line (011) 720 3145

A. How Well Did You Read The Passage?

1. What ailments or diseases do smokers over 65 years suffer?

2. What is the ration of cancer-related deaths between non-smokers and smokers?

3. Refer to paragraph 4, and briefly explain the mechanical evidence that smoking causes lung cancer

4. Mention 5 health anomalies that aggravate the incidence of heart attacks. How do you prove that air pollution is not the major cause of lung cancer?

5. Why does gaining weight after giving up pose less health problem than smoking?

6. Why the argument that many people would be jobless if everybody stopped smoking does not hold water?

7. If a couple that smokes a pack of 20 cigarettes a day save R3,900 per year, calculate how much per annum would be save by R3,900 smokers if they give up smoking?

8. Why are pipes and cigars not really safe?

9. What is an effective remedy for a smoker to reduce the risks of heart attacks?

B. How Many New Words Did You Learn?

1. A person who dies prematurely has died _____ than he/she was supposed to have died. (para 1)

2. A heart attack is fatal if it _____ a person. (para. 19)

3. The opposite of specific is _____ (para. 5)

4. Give an example of a health hazard other than gaining weight. (para. 13)

5. Give the synonym of "currently". (para 19)

6. Asthma is aggravated by smoke because it (irritates the eyes/worsens the asthma).

7. Ex-smokers are............. smokers. (para 21)

8. Is it true or false? "Will be spared death" means smokers will be killed by lung cancer. (para 21).

Unit 17
Forming of Adjectives

- Here are some examples of the use of suffixes in the forming of adjectives:

Suffix	Examples
-able	Loveable, valuable
-al	Critical, emotional
-(a) n	African, Chilean
-ant	Pleasant, triumphant
-ary	Customary, secondary
-ate	Fortunate, desperate
-ed	Baked, devoted
-ed	Contented, delighted
-en	Beaten, wooden
-ent	Dependant, despondent
-ern	Eastern, western
-ful	Beautiful, helpful
-ible	Reversible, terrible
-ic	Heroic, magnetic
-ing	Laughing. Interesting
-ish	British, Spanish
-ve	Attentive, instructive
-less	Valueless, hopeless
-like	Businesslike, childlike
-ly	Easterly, monthly
-ous	Courageous. Mountainous
-some	Wholesome, lonesome
-worthy	Blameworthy. Trustworthy
-y	Needy, might

29.1. Practising Activity

A. Form an adjective from each word within brackets:

A (wind) day	A (fault) plug
A (gold) opportunity	A (curl) tail
A (peace) man	A (destroy) dog
A (waste) person	A (wool) scarf
A (use) gift	A (storm) sea
A (fear) accident	A (quarrel) boy
An (admire) action	A (shine) floor
An angel bull	

B. Form adjectives from these words by using suffixes other than -ing or -ed, and then use each adjective with a suitable noun:

Success	Exception	Time
Norway	Lament	Danger
Trouble	Leisure	Move
Italy	Enthusiast	Supplement
Nature	Wonder	Scene
Sulphur	Help	Pity
Treachery	Week	Sweden

C. Pair each adjective with its correct meaning:

Plentiful	Occurring very often
False	A good looking
Capable	Not fertile
Barren	In great abundance

Handsome	At the exact time
Careless	Something not true
Frequent	Able to
Punctual	Not taking trouble to do things properly

D. Give the opposites of the adjectives in C above, and use the opposite in sentences that illustrate their meanings.

29.2. Improve Your Vocabulary

A. Choose the right meaning of each idiomatic expression.

a) A wild goose chase.

b) To smell a rat.

c) In nutshell.

d) To hit the nail on the head.

e) To always blow your trumpet.

Meanings

- To explain something in a few words.
- To be a boaster.
- To be suspicious of something wrong.
- Certain plans that have no chance of success.
- To say exactly right thing.

B. Explain the meaning of:

1. A local character.
2. Heading back.
3. A natural ridge.
4. To slope down.
5. A brow stew.
6. To clamber up.
7. Liable to bogging.
8. To look forward to.
9. To survey the site.
10. To feel proud.

C. Complete the following analogies:

1. Finger is to hand as toe is to…………
2. Metre is to length as kilogram is to………
3. North is to………as………east is to West.
4. Gun is to bullet as………is to arrow.

D. Replace the underlined phrases with one word which has the same meaning:

1. All of a sudden a shot rang out in the night.
2. His father did not want to listen to Bert's weak excuses.
3. Phyllis has been away from school for ten days.
4. Dad sat in a current of air and caught a chill.
5. School breaks up in two weeks' time for the Easter holidays.

E. Pair off the proverbs in Column A with their meanings in Column B.

Column A	Column B
Old birds are not caught with chaff.	A man with few needs which he can satisfy easily is a contented man.
Barking dogs seldom bite.	Forgive and forget
A man is known by his friends.	If you wish to catch a criminal employ another criminal to catch him.
Set a thief to catch a thief.	Be satisfied with your good fortune and do not examine the reasons too closely.
It is no use crying over spilt milk.	Those who threaten the most rarely carry out their threats.
Let bygones be bygones.	It is not easy to deceive those who are experienced.
Do not kill the goose that lays the golden eggs.	One's character may be judged by the company one keeps.
He is rich that has few wants.	It is no use regretting things which have been done and for which there is no remedy.

29.3. Reading and Reasoning Activity

Things You Pretend to Know

(And hope no one will ask)

Twentieth century civilization has fractured into countless areas of specialization. It would take a genius to stay abreast of the latest buzzwords, scientific breakthroughs and cultural references.

For example, do you know the difference between a gourmet and gourmand? Do you know where no man's land is or why a pig is in a poke? None of these terms is obscure, in fact, you've probably used them yourself without knowing what you were talking about.

Well, you can relax. Here are the facts you need to know to hold your head high in a dinner conversation, comprehend the evening news, and explain a thing or two to your 12-year-old nephew or at least understand him when he explains things to you.

1. What's the difference between a gourmet and a gourmand?

   Discretion. Pickiness. Taste. Knowledge. Put simply, a gourmet is a connoisseur of fine food and wine, a gourmand is one stop short of a glutton. Webster's kindly defines a gourmand as "one who is excessively fond of eating and drinking." Think Henry VIII, John Belushi, Marion Brando.

2. Why are liberals to the left and conservatives to the right?

   In 1789 the first French National Assembly was convened after the Revolution. The assembly was packed with 1,1777 deputies.

   As it happened, the liberal or radical members were seated to the left of the speaker, and the conservative members to the right. The practise spread, and the terms left wing and right wing arc still used round the world to denote the two political beliefs, liberalism and conservatism.

3. What makes a measure draconian?

   If it's harsh, brutal or too severe the circumstances, an act is considered draconian.

   The original Draco was a lawmaker in 7 Athens in the 7th Century BC. He published the first written laws in Greece, and is usually held responsible for the harshness of these laws, although Draco didn't create them – they were customs that Greeks had lived by for many years.

   Once their rules were in writing, many Greeks were appalled at how unreasonable the system was. Small thefts were punishable by death, and if a man couldn't pay his debts, he became a debt slave. Eventually the Greeks threw out Draco and "his" laws, cancelled all debts, treed the debt salves and created a new, more lenient set of civil rules.

4. Did the Three Musketeers actually exist?

   Only in the mind of Alexandre Dumas the Elder. He wrote the novel The

Three Musketeers in 1844. The setting is the 17th Century France, and the musketeers – Athos, Porthos and Aramis are swords-men who served King Louis XIII. Together they defeat Cardinal Richelieu in his plot to embarrass the royal family. The confusion about whether the musketeers were real arises because Louis XIII and Richelieu did indeed exist. But in common with many authors, Dumas used historical figures as foils for his fictional characters.

5. What makes someone a maven?

The airwaves are live with fashion mavens, wine mavens, and media mavens. Maven is Yiddish for "expert", but keep in mind that the word is often used sarcastically:

"Baseball mavens predicted the end of the strike this week, but the mavens struck out".

6. Where is no man's land?

During the Middle Ages, no man's land was located outside the north wall of the city of London, where the bodies of criminals were displayed. Since even minor crimes were punishable by death, there were plenty of bodies – hanged, beheaded, impaled-to serve as a warning to others.

Eventually a gallows was built inside the city proper. Years passed, and all round London land was settled and fields were cultivated – except for the former execution grounds which were claimed by no man. No man's land was the term used to describe the area, and only later, around 1900, was the phrase picked up in military parlance.

7. What is angst?

You're 14 and you've just realised you've bought the wrong kind of tackies. Or you're 24, and you don't know what you're doing with your life. Or you're 44, and you don't know what you're doing with your life.

Angst is German for "anguish" and signifies psychological suffering.

The word is sometimes prefaced by "existential" which gives a deeper, more troubled tone. If you suffer from existential angst, you don't need the tackies to turn you into an anguished puddle. The mere fact of existing in this world is torment enough.

8. What are flotsam and jetsam?

Flotsam and jetsam is a fancy way to refer to junk, waste or unimportant loose ends. The term refers to cargo from a ship that ends in the sea.

Flotsam is goods lost in a wreck that float on the water. Jetsam is goods thrown overboard (jettisoned) in order to stabilize a ship. Jetsam sinks.

According to maritime law, flotsam and jetsam forever belong to their original owner, but if someone else finds the stuff, he or she is entitled to a salvage award.

9. What is a pig in a poke?

A pig in a poke is an item or an idea that seems to be one thing but might well contain something different.

In medieval England, small pigs were sold at market in pokes, or little bags At times, however, some crafty farmers took to putting a cat in the bag and trying to sucker someone into buying the pig without looking inside the poke. If they looked, the farmer would warn, the pig might run away. Those sceptics who did look invariably "let the cat out of the bag".

By L. Padwa, *Everything you pretend to know and are afraid someone will ask*. Affinity Publishing, New York. 1996

A. How Well Did You Read The Passage?

1. Mention at least a year that falls under the twentieth century.

2. Give an example of:

    o The latest buzzword

    o A scientific breakthrough

    o A cultural reference

3. Was Henry VIII the gourmet or gourmand? Substantiate.

4. With which political beliefs is the left wing and the right wing associated?

5. Who were the three musketeers?

6. Give two reasons which made the three musketeers appear real.

7. Which people speak Yiddish?

8. What is the difference between flotsam and jetsam?

9. In one word what is a pig in a poke?

10. To let the cat out of the bag means.

B. How Many New Words Did You Learn?

1. To stay abreast is…………(para. 1)

2. Something is obscure if it is…………(strange, funny, unclear) (para. 2)

3. A glutton has a v………appetite.

4. Find the word which means the same as parliamentary representatives. (para.

5. A draconian rule is a…………rule. (para. 7)

6. The century is known as the Middle Ages. (para. 11)

7. According to military parlance what is no man's land? (para. 12)

8. Maritime relates to (military, sea, flotsam and jetsam) (para. 15)

9. Medieval England relates to (the England of Middle Ages, Sale of small pigs in bags, pig farming. (para 19)

10. Sceptic refers to (a doubting person, a person who buys small pigs, a person who buys small pigs, a person who lets the cat out of the bag). (para. 19)

Unit 18
The Infinitive

- It is a verb form expressing verbal notion without particular subject, tense etc.
- It may be used with or without "to":

a) "To" is omitted after

- Auxiliary verbs except "ought":

1. You will go.
2. He might see you.

b) these verbs: make, see, hear, dare, feel, need:

3. Did you see him come? (not to come)
4. We heard them go out.

- Infinitives are useful as a help in joining sentences. Sometimes "to" is used and sometimes it is not:

c) WITH "to":

1. I went to his house. I saw him.

   I went to his house to see him.

2. He would not do that. He is too honest.

   He is too honest to do that.

3. You must remember that. It is essential.

   It is essential for you to remember that.

WITHOUT "to":

1. The new man has arrived. I saw him.

   I saw the new man arrive.

2. The postman knocked. I heard him.

   I heard the postman knock.

30.1. Practising Activity

A. Join these sentences with the help of an infinitive (with or without "to"):

1. Alice has come. I asked her.
2. Thabo went. I heard him.
3. We missed him. We were sorry.
4. She helped you. I asked her.
5. I heard of your illness. I was very sorry.
6. An accident took at the comer. I saw it.
7. I cannot work any longer. I am much too tired.
8. Tom heard the good news. He was relieved.
9. Avoid making such mistakes. It is most important.
10. We must decide that first. It is essential.
11. Do not touch it. You have been warned several times.
12. This coffee is too hot. I can't drink it at the moment.

30.2. The Participles

- There are two types of participles, namely:

    1. The present participle, which always ends in -ing: running, singing etc.

    2. The past participle. Most past participles end in -ed, but there are many that are formed differently:

- talk > talked

- break > broken

- ring > rung

- shut > shut

NOTE WELL

An exhaustive list of past participles will be found in the ADDENDUM

- When used as adjectives, participles may be useful as an aid in joining sentences:

    1. I was going into a shop. I saw Nancy. Going into a shop, I saw Nancy.

    2. He lost his hat. He had to buy another. Having lost his hat, he had to buy another.

NOTE WELL:

Only sentences that have the same subject can as a rule be joined by using participles. The following sentences cannot be joined in this way as each sentence has a different subject:

1. He was loading his gun. A lion suddenly appeared.

We may combine these sentences in any of these ways:
- He was loading his gun when a lion suddenly appeared, or:
- As he was loading his gun, a lion suddenly appeared, NOT:
- Loading his gun, a lion suddenly appeared.

3.2.1. Practising Activity

- Join these sentences with the aid of participles:
    1. We see his difficulty. We sympathise with him.
    2. They have lost all their matches. They are very despondent.
    3. She opened the window. She saw the procession.
    4. I mowed the lawn. I took a well-earned rest.
    5. He kept under cover. He ran quickly.
    6. Tom ran across the playground. He sprained his ankle.
    7. You have broken one cup. You must not break another.
    8. He can advise you. He is in a position to know.
    9. I was walking down the street. I met Peter.
    10. You have won once. You might win again.

3.3.3. Improve Your Vocabulary

A. Find a meaning in Column B for each of the idiomatic expressions in Column A

Column A	Column B
(1) He sits on the fence	He was very busy
(2) He builds castles on the air	He save money for a time when it will be needed.
(3) He was at a loose end	That was the thing which spoilt what was otherwise perfect.
(4) He runs with the have and hunts with the hounds.	He tries to be friendly with both parties in a quarrel.
(5) He runs with the hare and hunts with the hounds	He became so excited that he did not know what he was doing.
(6) That added fuel to the flame.	He thinks about all the wonderful thing he hopes to be able to have or to do.
(7) That was the fly in the ointment	That made a bad situation worse.
(8) That is the goose that lays the golden eggs.	He refuse to decide one way or another.
(9) He had his hand full.	That is the thing that brings in a good deal of money.
(10) He had lost his head	He had nothing to do.

B. Choose correctly from each pair of words in brackets:

1. Continually borrowing from one's neighbour is a bad (habit, custom).

2. The two cars collided in the (centre, middle) of the street.

3. We sat down and rested in the (shadow, shade) of a tree.

4. His parents were (dissatisfied, unsatisfied) with his progress at school.

5. We have to turn out for rugby (practice, practise) at 16H00.

6. I do not know (weather, whether) he will be able to come today.

7. Last week the wind blew (continually, continuously) for three days.

8. He seldom or (ever, never) takes a holiday.

9. We had to describe (shortly, briefly) that we had seen at the pictures.

10. Her absence from school was (due to, owing to) illness.

C. Write short sentences that clearly show that each of the following has two or more different meanings:

1. head
2. sentence
3. state
4. page
5. lie
6. bark
7. bear
8. fair
9. leaves
10. second
11. bound
12. range
13. lists
14. round
15. plant
16. dart
17. scrub
18. bolt
19. mine
20. rest

D. Give one word for each of the underlined expressions.

1. The pie had a hard covering on the top.
2. The man who was attended to by the doctor was admitted to hospital.
3. The person who performs humorous performance on stage, television and in radio will be here today.
4. He took the top off the milk before he fed the cats.
5. The thief made his way like a snake round the corner.
6. This work is not compulsory.
7. The two bicycles were the same every respect.
8. The child was playing in the room for the use of young children.
9. Parliament is now having a meeting (…………is now in………)
10. How many students have written their names on the list signifying that they wish to attend (for) the course?

Words

- Session, similar
- Optional, slithered
- Enrolled, skimmed
- Patient, crust
- Nursery, comedian

E. Choose one of the words in brackets which matches the meaning of the words outside the brackets:

1. Change (alter, altar).
2. Jewellery (broach, brooch)

3. Raisin (current, currant)

4. Illegal (illicit, elicit)

5. Talent (flair, flare)

6. Glass cutter (glacier, glazier)

7. Golden (gilt, guilt)

8. Spirit (moral, morale)

9. Warlike (marshal, martial)

10. Crowded (popular, populous)

30.3. Reading and Reasoning Activity

How He Made It Against Odds!

1

It is not generally known that there are a very large number of extremely wealthy Africans in South Africa. In fact, there are, and have been, several millionaires.

When, for instances, the Koksatd herbalist, Mr Khotso, died in 1973 his estate was valued at millions of rands.

2

A typical case of an African businessman who, by his own endeavours, has amassed great wealth, is that of Mr Ephraim Tshabalala. Today his business interests have an annual turnover of more than R1.5 million, and he employs a considerable number of workers in his companies that sprang from his garage in Soweto. That very garage sells more petrol than any other in Southern Africa- and that includes all the African states south of the Sahara. The sole shareholders of all the companies are Mr Tshabalala and his wife.

3

Besides Tshabalala Motors, however, there are other money-spinners. Eyethu Cinema (Pty) Ltd, which sometimes has an audience of almost 5000 people, has been operative since 1969 and is the cornerstone of the entertainment available to Soweto residents. Tshabalala Dry Cleaners (Pty) Ltd owns two dry-cleaning concerns using the most up-to-date equipment available in the country.

4

Tshabalala Bazaars (Pty) Ltd, a self-service supermarket, is a large business which includes two butcheries and two restaurants. Mr Tshabalala also owns property in Swaziland, where he was born, to the value (in 1976) of R3 million. The controlling company is Tshabalala Enterprises which, like all the other companies, has an African Management Team.

5

This wealth has grown from humble beginnings. Mr Tshabalala started out in 1921 as a salesman in shoes and soft goods for a Johannesburg firm. A few years later he left to become a bus driver, then, in 1947, he opened a butchery with exactly R22 in his pocket and R1 2 which he borrowed from his wife.

6

While he ran the shop, he would cycle around the suburbs hawking pork bones and calves' heads. As his business prospered, he gradually expanded his undertaking until, today, he rules a financial empire.

7

"The opportunities are there," he says. "All a man needs to succeed, is ambition, honesty and perseverance. Only an indolent man sits down to bemoan his fate and to blame others for his failure in life. I am reminded," he adds, "of what Henry Ford, The famous American Car manufacturer once said: the most difficult part of becoming a millionaire is saving your first R100. After that you are on your way."

A. HOW WELL DID YOU READ THE PASSAGE?

1. How did Khotso become wealthy?

2. How do you know that Khotso was the millionaire?

3. What financial capital did Tshabalala get started his business empire?

4. How many businesses did that capital establish by 1976?

5. What is outstanding about Tshabalala Dry Cleaners (Pty) Ltd?

6. What did Tshabalala do before he started his business career?

7. What businesses are controlled by Tshabalala Bazaars (Pty) LTd?

8. Can you state the bottom line of becoming a successful businessman after you have studied Tshabalala as a millionaire businessman? Substantiate

9. How did Henry Ford of America influence Tshabalala's business career?

10. Back in 1987 saving RI 00 was equal to saving R100,000 today, how much would a serious South African investor save per day in order to make R100,000 after 12 months?

B. HOW MANY NEW WORDS DID YOU LEARN?

1. Find the word in para. 1 that means "very".

2. Give the two different meanings of estate. (para. 1)

3. Endeavours means (wealth, ups and downs, businesses) (para 2)

4. Amassed means (gathered, got, distributed)

5. What makes a business to be a cornerstone? (para 3)

6. Humble beginnings refers to ("strong, outstanding, lowly) beginnings.

7. Hawking pork bones means? (giving poor customers pork without charging money, selling pork at reasonable prices that could be paid by any person on the move) (para 6)

8. Prospered (became wealthy, got customers, became better) (Para 6)

9. What does the writer use for?

    a. Lazy

    b. Slowly or step by step.

    c. Riches

    d. People looking at or listening to some entertainment

    e. To ride on a bicycle.

10. For which type of business ownership does (Pty) Ltd stand for?

Unit 19
Proper Use of Modal Verbs

- CAN

    "Can" has two main uses:

    1. to express permission or possibility:

    You can come tomorrow.

    2. to express ability or capacity:

    I can drive a car.

- COULD

    "Could" is the past tense of "can"

    "Could" has the following uses:

    1. to express mere capacity:

    He could dance when he was young.

    2. to express permission:

    We could go on holiday when we finished writing our final examinations.

- MAY

    1. expresses permission:

    You may go with me if you wish.

    2. expresses possibility:

    We may find it useful.

- MIGHT

    As the past tense of "may", "might" expresses possibility:

    I thought that it might be useful.

    Therefore, when a possibility existed at a specified time in the past, but the possibility no longer exists, "might" and not "may" is used.

    He might have passed the examinations.

- MUST

    1. expresses compulsion or obligation:

    You must go.

- HAVE TO (Past Tense, HAD TO)

    1. may be used instead of "must" when the obligation or necessity is not so strong:

    You have to go.

- OUGHT TO

    1. denotes a duty or obligation:

    I know I ought to go, but I don't want to.

- SHOULD AND WOULD

    1. To express the future in the past,

    "shall" becomes "should", and "will" becomes "would":

    I shall enjoy it. I said I should enjoy it

    Zola will like it. He said that Zola would like it.

    "Should" and "would are used in subordinate clauses instead of "shall" and will" when the verb in the main clause is in the past tense as illustrated by the examples in (i) above. Here are some further examples:

    If he had been there, I should have asked him.

    I should tell you if I knew.

2. "Should" is used for all persons to express an obligation:

I should approach the bank manager.

You should go at once

3. When the verb in a main clause is hope, expect, or a similar word and it is in the past tense, "would" is used for all persons in the subordinate clauses:

He thought that we would agree.

I hoped that you would pass.

4. In request, "would" is more polite than "will" or a straight command:
Would you help me?

Would you mind closing the door?

31.1. Practising Activity

A. Complete these sentences by choosing the correct words:

1. (May, can) we ask you a question?

2. He (can, may) play chess very well.

3. It was late and I (have to, had to, must, ought to) leave.

4. He thought that he (can, could, may) do it.

5. He explained to me what (may, might) happen.

6. They asked me whether you (can, could, may) come.

7. He (may, can, could) be small, but he isn't a weakling.

8. She (can, could, might) play very well three years ago.

9. If you did not listen carefully you (might, may, should, would) have lost your way.

10. You (can, could, may, might) pour out the tea when it is ready.

B. Complete these sentences by filling in should or would:

1. I was sure you……..like it.
2. Don't you think that Kenny……….see it?
3. ……….you like another helping?
4. Did you think that he……….like it?
5. You……….ask him, I am sure that he…………..ask you if he were in your place.
6. The porter said that the train be……….late.
7. ……….you do your best to help her?
8. I thought that we……….be difficult.
9. Do you think that we……….accept his offer?
10. You……….think it over carefully.
11. Don't you think you……….?

31.2. Improve Your Vocabulary

A. What is the work of these people:

a. bricklayer

b. poulterer

c. shipwright

d. playwright

e. chauffeur

f. draughtsman

g. miller

h. usurer

i. auctioneer

j. architect

B. Write down one word for each of these expressions:

a. Look carefully and closely.

b. Small dirty pool of rainwater.

c. Ship able to travel below the surface of the sea.

d. Measure by means of a scale how heavy thing is.

e. Without any loss of time.

f. Go with someone.

g. Send goods to foreign countries.

h. Payment for the use of a house or of land.

i. Study of the stars.

j. That which cannot be digested.

Words

* Immediately	* submarine
* Accompany	* examine
* Indigestible	* rent
* Weigh	* puddle
* Export	* astronomy

C. Pair off the idiomatic expressions in Column A with the meanings in Column B.

Column A	Column B
(a) much the same.	* to talk round a subject, not to talk about the most important point.
(b) a bird's eye view.	* to be unpleasant, or bad-tempered.
(c) to beat about the bush	* in trouble.
(d) to give ear.	* very little different.
(e) to cut up rough.	* to listen to.
(f) in hot water	* general survey

D. Use these idiomatic expressions in suitable sentences:

a. Break new ground.

b. Hold one's own.

c. Lose heart.

d. More or less.

e. Pull oneself together

f. From time to time.

E. Complete these proverbs and use them in sentences of your own:

a. Well begun……

b. Least said……

c. Like father……

d. A fool and his money……

e. The early bird……

f. Honesty is the best……

g. Early to bed……

h. Dead men tell……

i. Enough is as good……

j. Spare the rod……

31.3. Punctuation

Punctuate the following conversation:

Hello Tony cried Cynthia Reynolds as they met in park avenue I see you ve got some toffees so that will save my having to buy them she exclaimed diving her hand into the paper bag which Archie hold out hi ! steady on yelled Archie with a frown don't take the whole bag!

31.4. Reading and Reasoning Activity

The Age of Social Engineering

Sure, life was cheap like a lie:

Statutes guided the native,

A statue claimed land like a fly,

Children studied history. There's a motive

For loyal citizens in fear of their birthright,

Who filled the vacant land with civilization,

And could, at will, display their might,

And unlike Christ, cherished affliction,

So Christ is true, others have asserted,

And now we witness its death

Made possible by the concerted

Effort for newspapers in mirth
The jazzy nights of District Six,
The Kofifi beat, no tricks.

By M. Kosani from Echoes of the Distant Oceans

A. Answer the following questions in full sentences:

1. Which period in the political history of South Africa would you say is the age of social engineering, and why?
2. Who are the natives of South Africa?
3. In the light of the age of social engineering, how was the native "guided" by statutes?
4. What is the purpose of studying of the South African history by children?
5. Did the study of South African history serve the purpose of history before 1994? Substantiate your point of view.
6. What is a citizen? Were the natives' citizens in South Africa during the age of social engineering? Substantiate.
7. In what way did the loyal citizens display their might?
8. To what does "its" in line 2 of stanza 3 refer?
9. Where is District Six? What happened to District Six during the Age of Social Engineering?
10. What is Kofifi? What happened to Kofifi during the Age of Social Engineering?

B. Study the figurative language and other poetic devices before you answer the following questions:

1. Identify and explain the figure of speech in line 1, stanza 1.

2. Briefly discuss the metaphor in line 2 to 4, stanza 1.

3. Identify and briefly discuss the figures of speech in stanza 2.

4. Compare and contrast the mood and the atmosphere between stanza 1–2 and stanza 3–4.

5. Briefly discuss how the rhyme of this poem contributes to the meaning of this poem.

6. Classify this poem and discuss briefly one of its main themes.

Unit 20
Homophones and Homonyms

32.1. Homophones

- They are words of the same language which are pronounced alike, but which differ in every other way:

(1) Air	Gaseous mixture mainly of oxygen and nitrogen surrounding earth, or atmosphere.
Heir	Person entitled to property as legal successor of its former owner
(2) All ready	All prepared or in readiness. (They're all ready and waiting for you.)
Already	By this time. (The train has already arrived.)
(3) Altar Alter	Table for a religious ceremony, to change
(4) All together	Everybody in one place
You'll find them all together	
Altogether	Completely, wholly, entirely
(it is altogether too difficult a problem)	
(5) Birth	Emergence of young from mother's body. (Mary gave birth to a healthy baby boy.)
Berth	Fixed bunk on a ship, train etc. for sleeping in.
(the birth in our compartment was stacked with suitcase)	

(6) Beach	Sandy shore of sea between high and low water mark. (Orient Beach in East London)
Beech	Forest tree with smooth bark and glossy leaves.
(7) Boar	Uncastrated male pig
Bore	Weary by tedious talk or dullness. (Some TV programmes bore me to death.)
(8) Bold	Confidentially assertive, adventurous, courageous (A bold leader inspires hope for better life.)
Bowled	In cricket deliver the all, dismiss batsman by delivering that (In the cricket match Makhaya Ntini bowled for over
sixty minutes	
(9) Brake	a device to slow down or stop a vehicle.
Break	To smash or fracture
(10) Cent	Coin of value, unit of currency
(a box of matches costs fifty cents)	
Scent	Pleasant odour or smell left by an animal (The scent of this perfume is feminine.)
(11) Cheque	Written order to bank to pay stated sum from drawer's account.
Check	Pause or test, examine, verify
(check the change before you leave the shop)	
(12) Chord	Straight line joining two points of a circle, in music, a Group of notes sounded together
Cord	Thick string
(13) Complement	Something that complete

In the sentence "He is wise", wise completes the meaning of the verb is and is said to the complement of is.)	
Compliment	Praise. (Teacher like to compliment a hard-working pupil)
(14) Course	Direction taken or intended, direction followed by river. Series of lectures, lessons in a particular subject etc.
Coarse	Rough or made of large particles, vulgar (of language)
(15) Corps	A military division, group of persons engaged in special activity (diplomatic corps)
Corpse	Dead human body
(16) Desert (des'ert)	Dry, desolate, region (Sahara region)
Desert (des'ert)	To leave or abandon
Dessert	Fruit and sweets eaten at the end of meal
(17) Dough	Thick mixture of flour and liquid for baking
Doe	Female of the hare, reindeer
(18). Fir	Evergreen coniferous tree
Fur	Short fine soft hair of certain animals
(19). Flea	Small wingless insect feeding on human and other blood
Flee	Run away from
(20). Lesson	Make or become less, diminish
(The employer decided to downsize some employees in order To lessen costs of running the company at a profit.)	
Lesson	Systematic instruction in subject, thing learnt by pupil, Experience that serves to warn or encourage.
(21) Main	Principal, most important, greatest, in size or extent (The main road in Queenstown is Cathcart Road.)

Mane	Long hair on neck of an animal especially horse or lion.
(22) Not	Expressing negation.
Knot	Intertwining of parts of one or more ropes, strings etc.
(23) Of	Preposition expressing origin or cause. (Paintings of Michelangelo)
Off	Adverbs meaning away, at or to a distance, (three miles off the main road)
(24) Plain	Easily understood, easy to perceive, outspoken, straight decorated, not intricate or decorated, level tract of land (The plain truth is, we are not unassailable by blame as humans.)
Plane	Make smooth with plane which is a tool for smoothing surface of wood
(25). Principal	Chief or most important
(Gold is south Africa's principal export)	
Principal	Leader head or chief person
(Mr Kosani is the new principal of our school)	
Principle	General basic law is not an excuse is not the hard and fast principle.)
Principle	A rule of conduct. (Always try to be fair), that is a Good principle to follow.)
(26) Quiet	Still and peaceful.
Quite	Wholly or entirely
(27) Reach	Get as far as, make contact with the hand or by telephone etc. (By noon we shall reach Magalisburg.)
Rich	Having much wealth, splendid, costly, elaborate, valuable, Abundant or ample.

(28) Sail	Travel on water by use of sail or engine-power, piece of Canvass extended on rigging to catch wind and propel vessels.
Sale	Exchange of goods or services for money, act of selling, occasion when goods are sold at reduced prices.
(29) Stationary	Still, motionless
Stationery	Paper, pens, notebooks, invoice books etc.
(30) Storey (our flat is on the fifth story of the building)	Floors into which a building is divided.
Story	Account of imaginary or past events, narrative, tale
(31) Tail	Hindmost part of animal etc.
Tale	Narrative or story
(32) Team	Set of players forming one side in game.
Teem	Be abundant, be full (the lake in our neighbourhood Teems with fish.
(33) Wander	Go from place to place aimlessly
Wonder	Be surprised to find, strange or remarkable thing.

Note Well

This is not an exhaustive list of English homophones.

32.2. HOMONYMS

They are words of the same language which are spelt and pronounced alike, but which differ in meaning

1. A bark of tree.

Dogs bark.

2. A bear is the dangerous animal.

He'll bear the consequences.

3. They lie in the shade.

To lie is sinful.

4. A safe way.

A steel safe.

5. To hail a taxi.

A hail storm.

6. Fine weather.

To pay a fine in court.

7. A heavy sentence for serious crime.

A simple sentence consists of a subject, verb and object.

8. To boil water.

A sore boil.

9. To tap lightly.

A leaky tap.

10. Ring a bell.

A gold ring.

11. To park a car.

A sunny park.

12 Sports ground.

Ground glass.

13. A firm hold.

A ship's hold.

14. To post a letter.

A wooden post.

To apply for the vacant post.

15. To draw water from the well.

To be well after illness.

16. To fell trees. (cut down trees)

He fell from the tree. (fell as past of fall)

A fell of an ox. (hide with hair)

A bushy fell. (a bushy hill)

17. South African fleet. (navy)

A fleet of cars.

A fleet movement. (fast movement)

18. To be fit for a job.

To fit the shirt.

To suffer a fit. (sudden seizure of epilepsy)

19. To miss a friend.

To miss the bus, opportunity.

Miss South Africa.

20. To be part of.

To part with.

21. Bill of exchange.

A bill of a bird.

To pay a bill.

Clean bill of health.

To pass a bill into law.

22. Bit by bit. (gradually)

The dog bit him. (bit past of bite)

23. Board of directors.

Go on board ship, aircraft etc.

24. To play darts.

Mosquitoes' dart.

25. Australia's down is suitable for sheep farming.

Down of birdlings.

To fall down.

26. A member of the bar. (banister)

To enjoy brandy in a bar.

A chocolate bar.

To bar a person in court proceedings.

27. To fold a paper, arms etc. The fold of Jesuits.

28. A gold mine.

This book is mine.

29. The human race.

To win a race.

30. A round shape.

A round figure.

To round off.

Round trips.

31. Cut with a saw.

Saw (as past of see).

32. An official seal.

A seal is an amphibious mammal.

33. A stalk of milk.

To Salk animals, enemy.

34. To stamp the floor.

To fix stamp on envelope.

35. To shoot with a gun etc.

Shoot of a tree, plant.

36. A wrist watch.

To watch a film, game etc.

37. Plot of a play, novel, story film.

To plot a crime.

Note Well:

This is not the exhaustive list of homonyms.

32.3. Show in sentences the difference between these pair of words:

1. All ready, already
2. All together, altogether
3. Boar, bore
4. Cent, scent
5. Corps, corpse

6. Desert, dessert

7. Fir, fur

8. Plain, plane

9. Quiet, quite

10. Stationary, stationery

B. Show in sentences that each of these words has two different meanings:

(i)	sentence
(ii)	spot
(iii)	post
(iv)	letter
(v)	lie
(vi)	fine
(vii)	rose
(viii)	desert
(ix)	movement
(x)	light

C. Choose the correct words from these within the brackets:

a. It is cool in the (shade, shadow) of the tree.

b. Calculate the distance from the (centre, middle) of the circle.

c. Drunken driving was the (cause, reason) of the accident.

d. The court declared the (marriage, wedding) invalid.

e. Our (voyage, journey) by ship to America took us three weeks.

f. (Lean, thin) cattle, cannot fetch a good price in the market.

g. He has (founded, found) his own private company after getting the proper (advise, advice) from the ECDC.

h. We normally (stay, live) at the Seaview Hotel during the festive season.

i. When it was his (turn, chance) to testify he refused.

j. I shall ask him to (lend, borrow) me his textbook.

32.3. Write down one word for each of these expressions:

a. Ending in death.

b. Advise against.

c. Burst with a loud noise.

d. Take part in contest.

e. Place for the burial of the dead.

f. Person who takes an examination for the purpose of obtaining a certificate of proficiency.

g. Wreath of flowers or leaves used as a decoration.

h. Road or track along which aeroplanes run before taking off and on which they land.

i. Animal or plant that lives on others.

j. Something that can easily be seen through.

WORDS

- Dissuade, compete
- Transparent, fatal
- Garland, explode
- Candidate, runaway
- Cemetery, parasite

32.4. Pair off the idiomatic expressions in Column A with their meanings in Column B, and then write sentences that illustrate the meaning of the idiomatic expressions.

Column A	Column B
a. stand on ceremony	Not providing for the future.
b. over and over	Speak plainly and bluntly
c. hand to mouth	Of one's own invention
d. take it into one's head	Be reserved and stiff
e. call a spade a spade	Reach a climax
f. rank and file	Repeatedly
g. come to a head	Suddenly think of an idea
h. out of one's head	Ordinary soldiers as contrasted with their officers (also used of the ordinary people in any movement, as distinct from their leaders)

32.5. Punctuate this passage

Alexander Graham Bell inventor of the telephone was born in Edinburg Scotland he and his assistant Thomas Watson were experimenting during the night of 2 June 1875 was down stairs and bell was upstairs suddenly Watson hear Mr Bell say quite clearly Mr Watson come here i want you this first speaking telephone consisted of an old cigar box sixty-one metres of wire and two magnets

32.6. Without changing their meaning, rewrite the sentences beginning with the underlined words:

a. Petrol is necessary for motor cars. Motor cars...

b. Books may be borrowed from a library. A library

c. A chemist usually sells pills. Pills may usually

d. Frank eras more than Eric. Eric's earnings are…

e. Hilda is shorter than Peggy. Peggy…

f. The National Road passes through Knysna. Knysna…

32.7. Reading and Reasoning Activity
Memories

The sun is rolling West

Leaving me to rest

With remembrances

And fragrances

She last wore. Instances

In her mellow

Voice bring the morrow.

Nor do I look sane

The morrow is the same,

No memories can caress

My tattered soul, endless

As the proverbial curse-

Dear angel,

My memories are pale.

To gaze the route of the boat,

My lass of a remote

Memory, in anguish

My soul doth relish

Her reverie to my rescue

And blessed is that sea view

A dozen days to share

With none, such a fair

Look, even a tourist

Can sight a spirit,

A delight of a pristine priest!

Waves cannot be the dirge

Nor her submerge.

Let the morning ascend,

And carols will blend

Our love. Those sprightly

Days still grace the lively

Memories till the lonely

Hours – so keen am I

To sing her a lullaby.

By M. Kosani from Echoes of the Distant Oceans

A. Use your dictionary to find out the meaning of the words used in this poem. You may also deduce their meanings from the context of the poem.

1. sane

2. caress

3. gaze

4. lass

5. anguish

6. relish

7. pristine

8. dirge

9. sprightly

10. lullaby

B. Answer the following questions in full sentences:

1. In one sentence, state what these memories are all about.

2. Mention any three things that are still vivid in the memories of this person about his lover.

3. What type of a person is this lover? Briefly explain.

4. Where has he last seen his lover?

5. Where do you think might have happened to this girl? Substantiate your point of view.

6. Discuss the effect of the imagery in Stanza 1 in relation to the mood and atmosphere of this poem.

7. Identify and explain the figure of speech in lines 1, 4 and 7, stanza 2.

8. What does the metaphor in line 6–7, Stanza 4 imply about the emotions of the speaker?

9. What does "cards" symbolize in line 2, stanza 5?

10. Discuss the rhyme of this poem.

Unit 21
Paraphrasing

- A paraphrase is a simple version of the original whereby a narrative or poetic text is reproduced in prose.

33.1. Rules for Paraphrasing

1. Read through the text and make a note of all unfamiliar words. Use your dictionary to find out the meanings of the unfamiliar words in the light of the context.

2. Now read the text keeping in mind the meanings of the unfamiliar words.

3. Make a note of any archaic words or phrases in common use today.

4. Follow the original, sentence by sentence and make a rough draft of your paraphrase. In doing this, you should keep points in mind:

    a) Keep to the style of the original as far as possible.

    b) Do not leave out any of the facts or ideas in the original. On the other hand, do not add any new facts or any ideas or explanations of your own.

    c) Do not change the person, number or tense of the original.

    d) Express questions or exclamations as statements.

    e) Translate figurative language into plain language.

    f) If any of the sentences in the original are long, substitute them with short sentences.

    g) Remember that as poetry is often condensed language, a paraphrase of verse is usually longer than the original.

    h) Eliminate rhyme and metre.

i) Compare the draft with the original to make sure that nothing has been lefty out.

j) Read your draft, without referring to the original, to make sure that it reads smoothly, and that it would be easily understood by anyone not having a knowledge of the original.

k) Prepare the final paraphrase, and check to see that it is properly punctuated, and that there are no errors of style.

33. 1.1. Examples of Paraphrase of Proverbs:

- Never look a gift horse in the mouth.

    Paraphrase: Do not examine too closely or be too critical of something that has been freely given to you.

- Do not cast pearls before swine.

    Paraphrase: Do not offer beautiful things to those who cannot appreciate them.

33.1.2. Practising Activity

Paraphrase this verse by using your own words as much as you can:

Beware of too sublime a sense of your own worth and consequence!

The man who dreams himself so great,

And his importance of such weight,

That all around in all that's done,

Must move and act for him alone, Will learn in school of tribulation

The folly of his expectation.

33.2. Summarising

- A SUMMARY IS THE SIMPLE AND SHORTER VERSION OF THE ORIGINAL TEXT.

33.2.1. Rules for Summarising

1. Use your own words for the important words from the original.
2. Omit everything that has no bearing or the main topic, and leave out the picturesque details e.g. The tail, hefty man whose neck was always decorated with gold chains from the reputable fashion houses, was declared bankrupt by the court.

   This would be abbreviated to read: The man was declared bankrupt.

3. Retain the names of the persons and places and dates.
4. Be concise, direct, simple and avoid repetition.
5. Use reported speech for direct speech.
6. Replace metaphorical expressions with literal language, unless they are necessary in the summary.

33.2.2. Practising Activity

- Summarise the passage to about one-third the length of the original. Think of a suitable title for the extract.

The Xhosa believe the Sangomas to be the contact between them and the spirits of their ancestors. They hold the key to the invisible world and are in constant communication with the spirits of the departed. The Sangomas are good people, devoted to the well-being of their people, putting right the wicked work done by sorcerers and evil doers and healing their victims. They differ from the herbalists who cure physical ailments, in that they are more concerned with a person's spirit.

Most of the complaints brought to the Sangomas are caused by the victim's neglect of the spirits of dead ancestors. The Sangomas will find out why the spirits are angry and will use their skill to pacify them.

Xhosa Sangomas may be of either sex. They wear white, a colour approved of by the spirits because it is the opposite of black, which symbolizes evil. On their heads, they wear bushy headdresses made of animal for and they usually carry some symbol of office, such as an antelope's horn or a switch made from a wildebeeste's tail. The type of animal for used is decided at the Sangoma's graduation. At that time they go into the forest alone and whatever animal they see first determines the skin used to make their headdresses. They also wear white beads on their right forearm to purify them and guard against evil spirits. The same applies to the white paint over their eyes and ears.

Perhaps the most interesting system Sangomas have of obtaining information is by using nomatotolo, or tiny messengers. These little spirits no bigger than walnuts are sent all around the world to gather knowledge. It is an eerie experience to consult a Sangoma who uses theses spirits. When one talks to such doctors they reply in high pitched, whistling voices which seem to come from the roof or the walls. Although many claim that this is done through ventriloquism no lip movements can be seen and the talking and the whistling occur simultaneously. These particular doctors are not common but people will go great lengths to obtain their services.

By Penny Miller: Myths and Legends of Southern Africa

33.3. Oral Activities

33.3.1. Telephone Calls

Discuss the correct method of making and receiving calls, and then arrange for pairs of learners to carry on conversations with each other.

Here are some possible topics:

- Ordering goods from a supplier.
- Reporting an accident to the police.
- Making an appointment.
- Enquiring about the times of bus departures.
- Reporting an electricity failure.
- Talking to the mother of a sick friend.
- Tactfully refusing an invitation.
- Booking a seat at a concert.
- Making enquiries about road conditions.

33.3.2. Radio Broadcasts

Learners should prepare short radio broadcasts and make the announcements. The rest of the class should discuss what was said and make suitable comments.

Here are a few suggested topics

- Weather report.
- A news item.

- An advertisement.
- Short announcement by a sports reporter.
- Announcement of the programmes for the next few hours.

33.3.3. Roving reporter

Learners should make turns as roving reporters, and interview different members of the class who should pretend to be one of the following:

- A visiting singer.
- A well-known medical specialist.
- A reformed ex-drug addict.
- A young successful entrepreneur.
- A famous South African soccer team.
- A famous defence attorney
- A mechanical engineer.

3.3.4. Giving directions

Choose a village, township or town well known to the learners, name certain streets, buildings or other places of interest and ask the learners to direct a stranger from one of them to the other, for example, from the place where a stranger is standing to the Airport, a named shop or a named street.

33.3.5. Speeches

Learners should from their groups select one of them to make speeches as follows:

- Imagine you are welcoming a visiting sports team to your school.

- Give a suitable reply as from the visiting captain.
- Propose a vote of thanks to a visiting speaker.
- Introduce a visiting speaker to a meeting.
- A farewell to a teacher who is leaving school.

33.4. Creative Writing

33.4.1. Short Story Writing

- Use any of the following plots as the basis of your story. Begin your story in an original way and make the ending surprising or unusual:

  a. A group of children accidentally start a forest fire. In their panic to escape the fire, they run away, but find themselves cut off by the flames. One of them realises that he must get through to the forest ranger to obtain help.

  b. A child computer genius accidentally gains access to the computer of a master criminal who is planning a bank robbery. As it is April Fool's Day, the police refuse to believe the story. The child decides to use his/her computer to foil the robbers.

  c. A violet orange glow appeared on the horizon and a few seconds later the dull sound of the distant explosion reached their ears.

  d. The last time we saw him, he was running frantically downhill with half the dogs of the village yapping at his heels.

33.4.2. Dialogue Writing

- When we write the actual words spoken by persons in dialogue form we do not use quotation marks. (inverted commas)

Get into pairs and write an interview with one of the following persons. Avoid questions which require straightforward yes, no or one-word answer. Then tape record the interview and play it to the class:

a. A successful pop star or TV personality.

b. A famous sportsperson.

c. Someone Who claims to have seen a UFO

d. The winner of a lotto.

33. 4.3. Folktale Writing

- Write a folktale connected with each title.
- The wolf and the jackal.
- The tortoise, the winner of the animal race.
- The jackal, the music teacher of the dove's chicks.
- The jackal and the animal lake.
- The friendship of the crocodile and the baboon.

33.5. Functional and Informative Writing

- A note on private/friendly/personal/informal letter

  1. The address of the writer is placed in the top right-hand comer together with the postal code number and the date. Each line is directly below the other. No commas or full stops.

  2. Then the greeting or salutation is written against the left-hand margin after you have left open one line. There is no comma.

  3. After leaving open one line below the salutation comes the body or subject matter which contains all the news. It is divided into paragraphs each

staring against the margin and separated by a blank space. All forms of punctuation must be appropriately inserted.

4. The ending or conclusion is written against the left-hand margin below the last paragraph after leaving open one line. No comma or full stop is needed.

5. The greeting and the ending differ according to whether you are writing to your parents, relatives, friends or strangers

- To parents and relatives begin and end thus:

(a) My dear Father	Your loving son Zola
(b) My dear Mother	Your loving daughter Liziwe
(c). Dear Zola	Your affectionate cousin Liziwe

- To friends, begin and end thus:

(a) My dear Foto	Yours affectionate Nomsa
(b) Dear Thando	Yours sincerely Diliza
(c) Dear Mr Davids	Your sincerely
Foto Mkalipi	

33.5.1. Now Write Any of the Following Letters

a. To your uncle who has sent you R200 as a birthday present. Thank him for his kind gift. Tell how you spent some of the money on an enjoyable party

b. Read the following letter carefully

27 Joubert Street
Queenstown 5319
20 November 2009

Dear Mr Jekwa

I wish to complain about the noise which has come from your home late every night this week. While I realise that you must practise your trumpet some time, I feel you ought to do it at a more suitable time. Ten o'clock in the evening is rather late to start playing. Even if you could play wee, the noise would still be unbearable at that time.

I hope that in future you will be a little more considerate of the feelings of others.

Yours sincerely

M Kosani

Now write a reply to this letter. You did not play the trumpet but on two or three occasions recently you have played some trumpet music on your Hi-fi system. You did not play music very loudly certainly not as loudly as Mr Kosani's television. You want to tell him this but you do not want to become enemies so you must be reasonably polite in your letter.

c. To your parents who are away from home. Write a letter to them describing a Bad storm and telling them of the damage caused in your garden and house.

d. To your father who is in hospital recovering from an operation. Tell him the Home News and try to cheer him up.

A. Note On Business/Formal Letter

1. The address of the writer is placed on the top right-hand corner together with the postal code number and the date. Each line is directly below the other. No commas or full stops.

2. Then below the writer's address one line is left open before the address

of the recipient is written against the left hand margin. No commas or full stops.

3. Then the salutation is also written against the left hand margin after you have left open one line. No comma is written.

4. After leaving one line below the salutation the heading in block letters is written. No full stop.

5. Below the salutation one line is left open before the subject matter is written in paragraphs. The content thereof should be brief, courteous and to the point. The style of language should be clear, straightforward and correct.

6. The ending or conclusion is written against the left hand margin below the last paragraph after leaving open one line. No comma or full stop is needed.

7. The salutation and the conclusion differ according to how you are acquainted with the recipient.

- If the salutation is:

Dear Sir/Madam, the ending is:

Yours faithfully, then signature, followed below it by initial and surname in block letters.

33.5.2. Write Any of These Business Letters

a. Write a letter to the manager of a factory or farm thanking him for organising a most enjoyable visit of your school.

b. To the Station Commander of your local police station reporting a drug-related crime. Give full details that shall lead to the arrest of the culprits.

c. You have seen an advertisement in your local Newspaper asking for applications for the post of an accountant. Respond by also enclosing your CV.

d. Your dog, which had strayed, was found and cared for by your local branch of the SPCA. Write to the person in charge, expressing your gratitude and offering your services as a voluntary helper.

e. Write to the editor of a Newspaper complaining about the closure of your local swimming pool.

33.6. Curriculum Vitae (CV) Writing

A CV is the brief account of a person's academic achievement, skills and job experience.

Its format is as follows

1. Personal Details

   1.1 Surname:

   1.2 Forenames

   1.3 Identity Number:

   1.4 Marital Status:

   1.5 Nationality:

   1.6 Residential Address:

   1.7 Postal Address:

   1.8 Driver's License:

2. Academic Achievement

2.1 Institution:

- Highest Grade Passed :
- Year Passed

- Subjects Passed ;

2.2 University:

- Degree Obtained
- Major Subjects
- Distinctions:

3. **Employment History**
   - Current Employer
   - Job description
   - Period of service
   - Job description
   - Skills acquired
   - Period of service

4. **Skills Acquired**

   It is wise and advantageous to list the skills that are relevant to your prospective employer and to briefly show how such skills could positively impact on the productivity.

5. **Declaration**

   I declare the particulars and information contained hereinabove is to the best of my knowledge true and correct.

BAPHUMELELE KOSANI

6. **References**

   It is advisable that you first request the referees' permission before you include them in your CV

33.6.1. Practising Activity

Read this biographical note and on the basis of it write the CV

Sandile Dumakude, the third person to have won the Fleur de Cap, one of South Africa's most prestigious acting award, six times, was born on the 18 September 1985 in Ginsberg, King Williamstown.

As the hardworking student and the able sportsman, especially in cricket and rugby, he won the bursary to study at Seibourne College in East London. He rose through the ranks to secure a place in the first team of the cricket.

After matriculating in 2000, he went to the University of Cape Town's drama school, where he was led to believe that he did not have enough talent to succeed as a professional actor.

He was working as a floor salesman for an interior design shop in Cape Town when one person who had noticed his talent invited him to join a small group of actors.

Dumakude spent some time in London at the London Mime School where, in addition to acting, he modelled bathing costumes.

Back in South Africa, he played in the controversial play Death of Hangman in 2004.

He also directed and lectured in drama at Stellenbosch University in 2006 and spent six months of 2007 in Johannesburg as a voice coach for the television series Egoli.

33.7. Informative Writing

33.7.1. Explain briefly how to perform any of the following operations

a. Programming a video recorder to record while you are out.
b. Programming a video camera to record any occasion

c. Setting up a computer programme.

33.7.2. Leave Clear Written Instructions

TO SOMEONE WHO IS GOING TO LOOK AFTER ONE OF THE FOLLOWING ANIMALS WHILE YOU ARE AWAY FOR A WEEK.

a. A large dog.

b. A pony.

c. A Siamese cat.

d. A tropical fish.

e. A tortoise.

33.7.2. Conduct a survey into the viewing patterns of the children in your school by means of a questionnaire like the one shown below. You may add more questions or change it in other ways to suit the requirement of your survey.

After the forms have been completed form groups to record the answers to the various sections or questions. You can record your findings in a pamphlet or a charts and groups.

If you have computers feed the data into a computer and record the findings on a printout.

Here is the model questionnaire:

STEPPING STONE HIGH SCHOOL

SURVEY OF CHILDREN'S TV VIEWING HABITS

Boy/Girl Grade.

Questionnaire

1. How many TV sets do you have at home?

   | 1 | | 2 | | 3 | | More than 3 |

2. Do you have a video recorder

   | Yes | | No |

3. Viewing habits SCHOOL HOLIDAYS WEEKENDS

   a. At which times do you usually watch TV

   4 pm–5 pm ☐ ☐

   5 pm–6 pm ☐ ☐

   6 pm–7 pm ☐ ☐

   7 pm–8 pm ☐ ☐

8 pm–9 pm □ □

Later than 9 pm □ □

b. About how time each week do you spend watching DVD or recorded programmes?

School days		Weekends		Holidays	
	Hours		Hours		hours

c. About how much time do you spend watching TV programmes each week?

Term time		Holidays	
	Hours		hours

4. Which kind of programmes do you prefer? (Give 1 to the kind you like most and 10 to the kind you like the least.)

Comedies ☐ Soapies ☐ Thrillers ☐ News ☐

Science fiction ☐ Documentaries ☐

Cartoons ☐ Educational ☐ Variety ☐

Pop Music ☐ Other ....

5. Which programmes do you never miss?

....
....

6. Which is your favourite programme?

When you have completed the investigation produce a written report in which the information is organized under separate headings and sub-headings. The following is a possible outline:

1. The purpose of the investigation.

2. How the data was obtained.

3. The detailed results of the survey.

4. A summary of the viewing patterns in each class.

5. A summary of the teachers' opinions.

6. Conclusions reached by your group.

7. Recommendations.

33.8. Spelling

RULE 3: When adding an ending beginning with a consonant, the final -e is retained

- Case   carefully, careless
- Hate   Hatefully, amuse, amusement
- Lone   lonely, loneliness

Some exceptions to the above rule are

- True   truly
- Argue   Argument etc.

RULE 4: Words of one syllable ending in a consonant preceded by one vowel double the final consonant when endings beginning with a vowel are added:

- Pat   patted
- Bit   bitten
- Rob   Robbing
- Fun   Funniest
- Wet   Wetter

RULE 5 : Words of more than ONE syllable in which the accent falls on the final syllable double the final consonant beginning with a vowel is added

- Refer   Referred
- Occur   occurred
- Commit   committing
- Allot   allotted
- Admit   admitted

If the accent does not fall on the final syllable, the consonant is not doubles

- Happen   happened
- Wonder   Wondered

RULE 6: When a word ends in y preceded by a consonant

a. Change the y into I and add -es when forming a plural noun or a singular verb:
   - Lady   ladies
   - Fairly   fairies
   - Bury   Buries

b. Change y into I and add -ed in the past tense
   - Carry   Carried
   - Bury   Buried
   - Pity   pitied
   - Copy   Copied

RULE 7: When a word ends in y preceded by a vowel, retain the y when adding -s, -ed or -ing

- Employ   employs/employed/employing
- Convey   conveys/conveyed/conveying
- Play   plays/played/playing

RULE 8: Words ending in -ery are likely to be Nouns and words ending in -ary are likely to be adjectives.

- Winery, refinery, artillery (Nouns)
- Secondary, Voluntary, imaginary (Adjectives)

33.8.1. Practising Activity

a. Add -ous to the following words : fame, continue, courage, pose, desire

b. Add -ful to the following words : fate, spite, use, hope, disagree, care

c. Add -s or -es, -ed, and -ing to the following words : annoy, deny, accompany, cry, study, journey, obey, play, spray, apply, pry, fry

d. Add -ery or -ary to complete the following words

Element-, legend-, deliv-,

Solit-, cemet-, green-,

Imagin-, machin-, ordin-,

Crock-, embroid-, boun-

e. Which word in each of the following pairs is spelt correctly?
1. sherif, sheriff
2. skilful, skilful
3. disapoint, disappoint
4. center, centre
5. celebrate, celebrate
6. jewelery, jewellery
7. baloon, balloon
8. ocurred, occurred
9. divelop, develop
10. salery, salary
11. all right, alright
12. colour, color
13. disolve, dissolve
14. measles, measless
15. parallel, parralell
16. vehical, vehicle
17. tobaco, tobacco
18. woolen, woolen
19. comittee, committee
20. prefered, preferred

Addendum A

Present tense	Past tense	Past participle
1. arise	Arose	Arisen
2. awake	Awoke	Awoken
3. bear (give birth to)	Bore	Born
4. bear (carry/support)	Bore	Borne
5. bend	Bent	Bent
6. bid	Bade (pron, bad)	Bidden/bid
7. bid (at an auction)	Bid	Bid
8. breed	Bred	Bred
9. broadcast	Broadcast	Broadcast
10. cast	Cast	Cast
11. catch	Caught	Caught
12. cling	Clung	Clung
13. come	Came	Come
14. cost	Cost	Cost
15. creep	Crept	Crept
16. cut	Cut	Cut
17. deal	Dealt	Dealt
18. dream	Dreamt. Dreamed)	Dreamt
19. dwell	Dwelt	Dwelt
20. feel	Felt	Felt
21. flee	Fled	Fled
22. fling	Flung	Flung
23. flow	Flowed	Flowed
24. fly	Flew	Flown
25. forbid	Forbade	Forbidden
26. forsake	Forsook	Forsaken
27. grind	Ground	Ground
28. hang (person)	Hanged	Hanged
29. hang (a thing)	Hung	Hung
30. hit	Hit	Hit
31. kneel	Knelt	Knelt

32. lead	Led	Led
33. lean	Leaned/leant	Leaned/leant
34. leap	Leapt	Leapt
35. learn	Learned/learnt	Learned/learnt
36. leave	Left	Left
37. let	Let	Let
38. lie (down)	Lay	Lain
39. lie (tell an untruth)	Lied	Lied
40. light	Lit/lighted	Lit/lighted
41. mean	Meant	Meant
42. throw	Threw	Thrown
43. tread	Trod	Trodden
44. wake	Woke	Woken
45. wear	Wore	Worn
46. weave	Wove/weaved	Woven/weaved
47. weep	Wept	Wept
48. wet	Wet	Wet
49. win	Won	Won
50. wind	Wound	Wound
51. wring	wrung	Wrung

Addendum B

SELECTED LIST OF ABBREVIATIONS

1. A/C	Account
2. ACDP	African Christian Democratic Part.
3. AD	Anno Domini) in the year of our Lord.
4. am	(Ante meridian) before noon.
5. ANC	African National Congress
6. anc	antenuptial contract
7. anon.	anonymous
8. approx.	approximately
9. BA	Bachelor of Arts
10. BC	Before Christ
11. BCom	Bachelor of Commerce
12. BEE	Black Economic Empowerment
13. BSc	Bachelor of Science
14. ch	chapter
15. chq	cheque
16. Co	Company
17. c/o	Care of/Corner of
18. Cr	Credit side of general ledger
19. Dept	Department
20. doz	dozen
21. DP	Democratic Party
22. Dr	Doctor/Drive/debit side of general ledger
23. ea	each
24. EC	Eastern Cape
25. e.g.	(exempli gratia) for example
26. etc.	(et cetera) and other things.
27. fob	free OH board (a ship)
28. ft.	feet
29. GMT	Greenwich Mean Time

30. GPO	General Post Office
31. hp	hire purchase/horse power
32. i.e.	(id est) that is
33. IFP	Inkatha Freedom Party
34. KC/QC	King's Counsel/Queens Counsel
35. KZN	KwaZulu Natal
36. LCM	lowest common multiple
37. LLB	Bachelor of Laws
38. Ltd	limited
39. MA	Master of Arts
40. Max.	Maximum
41. MCom	Master of Commerce
42. MEC	Member of Executive Council
43. Messrs	Messieurs (plural of Mr)
44. Min	Minimum/Minister
45. MP	Member of parliament
46. MSc	Master of science
47. NB	(Nota bene) note well
48. NCOP	National council of provinces
49. NEC	National executive council
50. No	Number
51. oz	Ounce
52. pa	(per annum) each year
53. PAC	Pan Africanist congress
54. par	Paragraph
55. per cent	For each hundred
56. PLO	Palestine liberation organisation
57. pm	(post meridian) after noon
58. po	Post office
59. Prof	Professor
60. PS	Post scriptum (something added to a letter after signature
61. PSA	Public servants Association (a trade union)
62. PTO	Please Turn Over (The Page)
63. Rd	Road
64. Rev	Reverend
65. RIP	(requiescat in pace) may he/she rest In peace

66. RSVP	(re' pondez s'il vous plait) please reply
67. SAAF	South African Air force
68. SAB	South African brewery
69. SABC	South African broadcasting corporation
70. SABS	South African bureau of standards
71. SANDF	Sout African national defence force
72. SAPS	South African police service
73. Sen	Senior/senator
74. SOS	"Save our Souls" (a distress signal)
75. SPCA	Society for the prevention of cruelty to animals
76. St	Street/saint
77. Tel No	Telephone number
78. UK	United kingdom of Great Britain
79. USA	Unites states of America
80. Via	By way of
81. Viz	(videlicet) namely
82. vol	Volume
83. vs	Versus/against
84. xmas	Christmas
85. YMCA	Young men's Christian Association

Addendum C

SELECTED LIST OF ACRONYMS

® Acronyms arc the initial letters of abbreviations which have become words in themselves-

1. ABSA	Amalgamated Banks of South Africa
2. ASGISA South	The Accelerated and Shared Growth Initiative in Africa (The South African economic plan introduced by
The	Mbeki Government)
3. BODMAS subtraction.	brackets, of, division, multiplication, addition,
4. COSATU	Congress of South African Trade Unions
5. ESKOM	Electricity Supply Commission (Kommissie)
6. ISCOR	Iron and Steel Corporation
7. LIFO	Last in first out (a rule of fair labour practice in respect of retrenchment)
8. NASA	National .Aeronautics and Space Administration
9. NAPTOSA of South	National Professional Teachers' Organisation
Africa	Bachelor of Commerce
10. RADA	Royal Academy of Dramatic Arts
11. SADTU	South African Democratic Teachers Union
12. SALT	Strategic Arms Limitation Talks
13. SANTA	South African Tuberculosis Association
14. SOWETO	South Western Townships
15. Telkom	Telecommunication Commission (Kommissie)
16. UNISA	University of South Africa

Addendum D

ANTONYMS/OPPOSITES

1. cold	Hot
2. dry	Wet
3. love	Hate, hatred
4. question	Answer
5. asleep	Awake
6. front	Back
7. joy	Sorrow, grief
8. begin	End, cease
9. friend	Enemy, foe
10. dead	Alive
11. busy	Idle
12. sweet	Sour, acid, bitter
13. bright	Dull
14. rise	Fall, sink
15. true	False
16. quick	Slow
17. start	Finish
18. ugly	Beautiful
19. near	Far, distant
20. kind	Cruel
21. empty	Full
22. ever	Never
23. bless	Curse
24. adult	Child
25. North	South
26. East	West
27. high	Low
28. upper	Lower
29. better	Worse

30. entrance	Exit
31. active	Passive
32. noise	Silence
33. quiet	Noisy
34. inner	Outer
35. lend	Borrow
36. go	Come
37. hard	Soft
38. old	New
39. junior	Senior
40. live	Die
41. long	Short
42. enjoy	Dislike
43. rejoice	Mourn-, grieve
44. pleasant	Disagreeable
45. success	Failure
46. harmony	Discord
47. blessing	Disaster
48. generous	Mean, selfish
49. valour	Cowardice
50. bravery	Cowardice
51. advance	Retire, retreat
52. arrive	Depart/leave
53. attack	Defend
54. before	Behind/after
55. engage	Dismiss
56. appear	Vanish/disappear
57. everywhere	Nowhere
58. collect	Disperse
59. modern	Ancient
60. former	Latter
61. least	Greatest
62. slender	Stout
63. robust	Feeble, delicate
64. smart/clever	Foolish/stupid
65. all	None

66. often	Seldom
67. fresh	Stale
68. straight	Crooked
69. deep	Shallow
70. praise	Blame
71. wild	Tame
72. profit/gain	Loss
73. lead	Follow
74. public	Private
75. acute	Obtuse
76 lazy	Industrious
77. arrive	Depart
78. remember	Forget
79. knowledge	Ignorance
80. pale	Ruddy
81. raw	Cooked
82. accept	Reject/refuse
83. polite	Rude
84. summit	Base
85. apex	Base
86. dawn	Dusk
87. ascend	Descend
88. vacant	Occupied
89. hope	Despair
90. interior	Exterior
91. obey	Command
92. conceal	Reveal
93. foreign	Native
94. smile	Frown/angry
95. wax	Wane
96. prosperity	Adversity
97. victory	Defeat
98. superior	Inferior
99. level	Steep
100. liquid	Solid
101. pardon	Punish

102. complainant	Defendant
103. debtor	Creditor
104. rural	Urban
105. emigrant	Immigrant
106. optimist	Pessimist
107. numerous	Sparse
108. transparent	Opaque
109. pedestrian	Passenger
110. guilty	Innocent
111. ancestor	Progeny
112. assemble	Disperse
113. condemn	Exonerate
114. slim	Stout
115. lawful	Unlawful/illegal
116. attract	Distract
117. amateur	Professional
118. confine	Release
119. pure	Impure/adulterated
120. lovely	Repulsive
121. theory	Practice
122. hostile	Friendly
123. real	Imaginary
124. level	Steep
125. prosperity	Adversity
126. victory	Defeat
127. superior	Inferior
128. stationary	Moving
129. dymanic	Static
130. spacious	Limited
131. sober	Intoxicated/drunk
132. abundance	Scarcity
133. common	Rare
134. simple	Complex
135. barren	Fertile/fruitful
136. ally	Enemy
137. fiow	Ebb

138. familiar	Strange
139. extravagant	Thrift
140. virtue	Vice
141. wisdom	Folly
142. within	Without
143. polite	Rude
144. agree	Disagree/contradict

Addendum E

SYNONYMS

1. abandon	Desert/forsake/leave
2. abbreviate	Curtail/abridge/compress
3. abundant	Ample/copious/plentiful
4. adore	Worship/idolise
5. alive	Lively/vivacious
6. ally	Colleague/partner/helper
7. amend	Improve/ameliorate
8. assent	Consent/agree/acquiesce
9. bad	Evil/wicked/devilish
10. beautify	Adorn/decorate
11. big	Enormous/huge/great/vast gigantic/ mighty/large/bulky/majestic
12. blame	Reprove/Censure
13. blessing	Benediction/benison
14. brave	Courageous/daring/fearless/intrepid
15. bright	Clear/brilliant/lustrous/transparent! Intelligent -» ;.
16. brittle	Frail/fragile -» ;.
17. burglar	Thief/bandit/brigand/highwayman
18. busy	Active/alert/lively/nimble/diligent/ industrious
19. catch	Capture/arrest/seize/apprehend
20. cause	Reason/purpose/motive
21. charity	Philanthropy/benevolence
22. choose	Select/discriminate/differentiate
23. clever	Ingenious/versatile/precocious
24. clothe	Attire/dress/garb/apparel/raiment
25. confess	Admit/acknowledge
26. cruelty	Oppression/tyranny/persecution

27. dangerous	Risky/perilous/hazardous
28. dear	Costly/expensive
29. decrease	Reduce/lessen/contract/diminish/curtail
30. difficult	Hard/intricate/complex
31. disaster	Misfortune/calamity/adversity/catastrophe
32. discourse	Lecture/dissertation/sermon/exhortation
33. disease	Sickness/ailment/malady
34. disfigure	Deface/injure/mar
35. dishonest	Deceitful/deceptive/fraudulent/unjust/unscrupulous
36. disorder	Chaos/confusion
37. dull	Gloomy/dreary/melancholy/cheerless
38. eager	Keen/enthusiastic
39. earn	Achieve/gain/win/acquire/merit
40. eject	Expel/emit/cast/dislodge
41. elevate	Lift/improve/raise/heighten
42. elude	Baffle/fool/cheat/avoid
43. emancipate	Free/liberate/release
44. embrace	Hug/clasp/include
45. emotion	Feeling/passion
46. enemy	Foe/opponent/adversary/antagonist
47. enough	Sufficient/adequate
48. enquire	Examine/explore/seek/search/investigate/pry/inspect
49. entice	Lure/persuade/allure
50. entire	Whole/total
51. eradicate	Eliminate/exterminate/destroy
52. esteem	Admire/value/prize/honour
53. external	Perpetual/infinite/ceaseless
54. exaggerate	Enlarge/overstate/heighten/amplify
55. excess	Surplus/increase
56. famous	Eminent/renowned/celebrated/distinguish

57.	fashion	Style/form/custom/
58.	fatal	Deadly/mortal
59.	fate	Destiny/end
60.	fault	Error/flaw/defect/mistake
61.	fear	Terror/dread
62.	fearful	Frightened/faint - hearted/cowardly/timid/nervous
63.	fight	Battle/conflict/strife/combat/contest/struggle/contention
64.	firm	Durable/lasting/substantial/binding
65.	fond	Loving/devoted/' affectionate
66.	frank	Open/sincere/plain/outspoken
67.	friend	Companion/associate/colleague/comrade
68.	frugal	Economical/thrifty/sparing
69.	fruitful	Fertile! productive/prolific
70.	game	Sport/recreation/pastime/fun/frolic
71.	gay	Merry/jolly/lively/blithe/cheerful/fun
72.	gaze	Stare/espy/peer/reconnoitre M
73.	general	Universal/common
74.	generous	Kind/big-hearted/liberal/noble
75.	genuine	Pure/real
76.	good	Just/true/righteous/virtuous/upright
77.	habit	Custom/usage/way
78.	hateful	Detestable/abominable
79.	help	Assist/aid/support
80.	high	Tall/lofty/elaborate
81.	hinder	Impede/obstruct/thwart
82.	home	Dwelling/residence/abode/habitation
83.	increase	Enlarge/argument/extend/expand/amplify
84.	infinite	Endless/everlasting/boundless ' limitless/eternal/
85.	injure	Hurt/harm/violate/wrong/ill- treat/damage
86.	insolvent	Bankrupt

87. invasion	Attack/raid
88. invoke	Call I summon
89 irritate	Tease/provoke
90 kind	Good/considerate/tender/affectionate/thoughtful
91 lazy	Idle/indolent/inactive/sluggish
92 lure	Entice/seduce/beguile/coax/persuade
93 map	Plan/chart/sketch/outline/design
94 mistake	Fault/error/blunder/
95 motive	reason/purpose
96 narrative	say/report/recount/tell
97 necessary	essential/needful/requisite
98 obey	submit/yield
99 obedient	submissive/respectful/meek/servile
100 obscene	impure/indecent
101 obsolute	old/ancient/antique
102 oral	verbal I unwritten
103 oratory	eloquence/rhetoric
104 patron	Supporter
105 Polite	well - behaved/well-bred/courteous/civil/polished
106 poor	destitute/needy
107 port	Harbour
108 praise	applaud/compliment
109 pretty	beautiful/neat/attractive/lovely/fine/gorgeous
110 proclaim	advertise/broadcast/propagate
111 quiet	calm/still/serene/placid/tranquil
112 rash	careless/reckless/tactless/indiscreet
113 Rude	impolite/insolent/abrasive/offensive
114 Real	genuine/original/authentic
115 safe	protected/secure/guarded
116 scorn	condemn/despise/abhor
117 See	view/behold/perceive/discern
118 small	condemn/despise/abhor

119 Smell	little/tiny
120 smooth	plain/level/uneven
121 spread	distribute/diffuse/disseminate/disperse/broadcast
122 strong	powerful/robust/sturdy/stalwart
123 suitable	appropriate/befitting/becoming
124 surrender	capitulate/submit/yield/relinquish
125 timid	fearful/fain-hearted/cowardly
126 trick	hoax
127 try	attempt/strive/endeavour
128 ugly	repulsive/grotesque/hideous/uncouth/horrid/
129 value	worth/esteem/appreciate
130 victory	success/triumph
131 weak	frail feeble/impotent^

Addendum F

ASSOCIATED WITH CERTAIN ADJECTIVES NOUNS

1 ships	Nautical, navel
2 spring	vernal
3 winter	brumal
4 mother	material
5 father	paternal
6 sister	sororal
7 brother	fraternal
8 son	filial
9 daughter	filial
10 servant	menial
11 shepherd	pastoral
12 morning	Material
13 day	diurnal
14 night	nocturnal
15 love	erotic
16 marriage	Nuptial, conjugal
17 earth	terrestrial
18 heaven	celestial
19 seeing	Visual, optical
20 hearing	Aural, auditory
21 smelling	olfactory
22 sound	acoustic
23 water	aquatic
24 sea	Marine, maritime
25 air	pneumatic
26 land	Praedial (legal term)
27 moon	lunar
28 sun	solar
29 stars	Steller

30 river	fluvial
31 brain	cerebral
32 heart	cardiac
33 tongue	glossal
34 throat	guttural
35 gums	gingival
36 lips	Labial
37 nose	Nasal
38 lungs	pulmonary
39 money	Fiscal, pecuniary
40 milk	lacteal
41 weaving	textile
42 kitchen	culinary
43 town/city	Urban
44 country	Rural, rustic
45 old age	senile

Addendum G

DIMINUTIVES

1. ball	Ballet, bullet
2. book	Booklet
3. brace	Bracelet
4. cask	Casket
5. cigar	Cigarette
6. corn	Kernel
7. crown	Coronet
8. dear	Darling
9. drop	Droplet
10. duck	Ducking
11. eagle	Eaglet
12. flower	Floweret
13. goose	Gosling
14. grain	Granule
15. hill	Hillock
16. ice	Icicle
17. lamb	Lambkin
18. lance	Lancet
19. lass	Lassie
20. latch	Latchet
21. leaf	Leaflet
22. lock	Locket
23. man	Manikin
24. park	Paddock
25. part	Particle
26. ring	Ringlet
27. river	Rivulet
28. sack	Satchel
29. scythe	Sickle

30. seed	Seedlet/seedling
31. spark	Sparklet
32. speck	speckle
33. statue	Statuette
34. stream	streamlet
35. tower	Turret
36. verse	Versicle

Addendum H

GENDER

	MASCULINE	FEMININE
1.	Actor	Actress
2.	bachelor	Spinster
3.	best man	Bridesmaid
4.	bridegroom	Bride
5.	bull	Cow
6.	cock	Hen
7.	dog	Bitch
8.	duke	Duchess
9.	earl	Countess
10.	father-in-law	Mother-in-law
11.	heir	Heiress
12.	hero	Heroine
13.	host	Hostess
14.	lad	Lass
15.	lion	Lioness
16.	lord	Lady
17.	male	Female
18.	mayor	Mayoress
19.	monk	Nun
20.	peacock	Peahen
21.	poet	Poetess
22.	postmaster	Postmistress
23.	ram (sheep)	Ewe
24.	sir	Madam
25.	stallion (horse)	Mare
26.	waiter	Waitress
27.	widower	widow

Addendum I

FORMATION OF NOUNS FROM OTHER WORDS

WORD	NOUN
1. Weigh	Weight
2. high	Height/highness
3. fix	Fixture
4. mix	Mixture
5. depart	Departure
6. moist	Moisture
7. wide	Width
8. broad	Breadth
9. deep	Depth
10. young	Youth
11. true	Truth
12. strong	Strength
13. long	Length
14. warm	Warmth
15. die	Death
16. busy	Business
17. kind	Kindness
18. dry	Dryness
19. holy	Holiness
20. short	Shortness
21. sharp	Sharpness
22. sad	Sadness
23. new	Newness
24. round	Roundness
25. room	Roominess
26. tender	Tenderness
27. tire	Tiredness
28. steal	Stealthiness

29. white	Whiteness
30. weary	Weariness
31. heart	Heartiness
32. light	Lightness
33. large	Largeness
34. low	Lawness
35. lazy	Laziness
36. love	Loveliness
37. loud	Loudness
38. hard	Hardness
39. forgetful	Forgetfulness
40. fond	Fondness
41. fearless	Fearlessness
42. bold	Boldness
43. bright	Brightness
44. clean	Cleanliness
45. coarse	Coarseness
46. black	Blackness
47. drunk	Drunkenness
48. deaf	Deafness
49. noble	Nobility
50. honest	Honesty
51. prosper	Prosperity
52. punctual	Punctuality
53. loyal	Loyalty
54. pure	Purity
55. cruel	Cruelty
56. able	Ability
57. regular	Regularity
58. anxious	Anxiety
59. timid	Timidity
60. absurd	Absurdity
61. gay	Gaiety
62. simple	Simplicity
63. real	Reality
64. probable	Probability

65. very	Variety'
66. severe	/Severity
67. sincere	Sincerity severance
68. wise	Wisdom
69. king	Kingdom
70. free	Freedom
71. child	Childhood
72. false	Falsehood
73. neighbour	Neighbourhood
74. boy	Boyhood
75. man	Manhood
76. woman	Womanhood
77. god	Godhood
78. bag	Baggage
79. bond	Bondage
80. mile	Mileage
81. rough	Roughage
82. carrier	Carriage
83. pass	Passage
84. short	Shortage
85. marry	Marriage
86. govern	Government
87. move	Movement
88. employ	Employment
89. appoint	Appointment
90. argue	Argument
91. pronounce	Pronouncement
92. merry	Merriment
93. Judge	Judgement
94. destroy	Destruction
95. intend	Intention
96. extend	Extension
97. accommodate	Accommodation
98. explain	Explanation
99. reveal	Revelation
100. invade	Invasion

101. provide	Provision
102. submit	Submission
103. vary	Variation/variety
104. satisfy	Satisfaction
105. possess	Possession
106. permit	Permission
107. prevent	Prevention
108. persuade	Persuasion
109. prepare	Preparation
119. organise	Organisation
111. instruct	Instruction
112. immigrate	Immigration
113. inspect	Inspection
114. imagine	Imagination
115. infect	Infection
116. explode	Explosion
117. expect	Expectation
118. edit	Edition
119. describe	Description
120. divide	Division
121. contribute	Contribution
122. conclude	Conclusion
123. compete	Competition
124. admire	Admiration
125. attract	Attraction
126. recognise	Recognition
127. receive	Reception/receipt
128. ventilate	Ventilation
129. absent	Absence
130. endure	Endurance
131. enter	Entrance
132. differ	Difference
133. defend	Defence
134. grieve	Grievance
135. innocent	Innocence
136. instant	Instance

137. important	Importance
138. hinder	Hindrance
139. neglect	Negligence
140. observe	Observance
141. ignore	Ignorance
142. perform	Performance
143. fragrant	Fragrance
144. candid	Candour
145. ardent	Ardour
146. splendid	Splendour
147. save	Saviour
148. behave	Behaviour
149. fell	Failure
150. seize	Seizure
151. please	Pleasure
152. friend	Friendship
153. member	Membership
154. lead	Leadership
155. hard	Hardship
156. arrive	Arrival
157. deny	Denial
158. bury	Burial
159. hero	Heroism
160. capital	Capitalism
161. communal	Communism
162. criticise	Criticism
163. serve	Service
164. just	Justice
165. analyse	Analysis
166. synthesise	Synthesis
167. lose	Loss
168. know	Knowledge
169. think	Thought
170. join	Joint
171. conquer	Conquest
172. proud	Pride

173. prove	Proof
174. draw	Draught
175. sell	Sale
176. awful	Awe
177. lend	Loan
178. solitary	Solitude
179. slave	Slavery
180. poet	Poetry
181 coal	colliery

Addendum J

ADJECTIVES FORMED FROM OTHER WORDS

WORD	ADJECTIVE
1. favour	Favourable
2. honour	Honourable
3. charity	Charitable
4. pity	Pitiable
5. jove	Lovable
6. notice	Noticeable
7. memory	Memorable
8. comfort	Comfortable
9. respect	Respectable
10. justice	Justifiable
11. imagine	Imaginable
12. laugh	Laughable
13. move	Movable
14. compare	Comparable
15. proof	Provable
16. prevent	Preventable
17. pass	Passable
18. pronounce	Pronounceable
19. please	Pleasurable
20. pursue	Perusable
21. remove	Removable
22. recognise	Recognisable
23. shape	Shapable
24. vary	Variable
25. marry	Marriageable
26. argue	Arguable
27. account	Accountable
28. believe	Believable

29. advise	Advisable
30. neglect	Negligible
31. divide	Divisible
32. fail	Fallible
33. force	Forcible
34. sense	Sensible
35. office	Official
36. essence	Essential
37. ceremony	Ceremonial
38. benefit	Beneficial
39. habit	Habitual
40. equator	Equatorial
41. palace	Palatial
42. nature	Natural
43. choir	Choral
44. parent	Parental
45. occasion	Occasional
46. nation	National
47. comic	Comical
48. season	Seasonal
49. poet	Poetical
50. accident	Accidental
51. danger	Dangerous
52. joy	Joyous
53. mountain	Mountainous
54. study	Studious
55. prosper	Prospers
56. continue	Continues
57. mischief	Mischievous
58. disaster	Disastrous
59. courage	Courageous
60. victory	Victorious
61. vigour	Vigorous
62. caution	Cautious
63. fame	Famous
64. adventure	Adventurous

65. instant	Instantaneous
66. glory	Glorious
67. luxury	Luxurious
68. venom	Venomous
69. space	Spacious
70. suspect	Suspicious
71. rebel	Rebellious
72. injure	Injurious
73. attract	Attractive
74. compete	Competitive
75. argue	Argumentative
76. represent	Representative
77. compare	Comparative
78. defend	Defensive
79. describe	Descriptive
80. effect	Effective
81. infect	Infective
82. imagine	Imaginative
83. persuade	Persuasive
84. receive	Receptive
85. talk	Talkative
86. punish	Punitive
87. decide	Decisive
88. conclude	Conclusive
89. extend	Extensive
90. watch	Watchful
91. help	Helpful
92. true	Truthful
93. power	Powerful
94. plenty	Plentiful
95. neglect	Neglectful
96. mourn	Mournful
97. hope	Hopeful
98. faith	Faithful
99. harm	Harmful
100. forget	Forgetful

101. law	Lawful
102. force	Forceful
103. fear	Fearful
104. boast	Boastful
105. beauty	Beautiful
106. child	Childish
107. devil	Devilish
108. dry	Dryish
109. dog	Doggish
110. fool	Foolish
111. flat	Flatish
112. fond	Loudish
113. round	Roundish
114. red	Reddish
115. self	Selfish
116. white	Whitish
117. sheep	Sheepish
118. wood	Wooden
119. gold	Golden
120. wool	Woollen
121. drunk	Drunken
122. earth	Earthen
123. ash	Ashen
124. Emphasise	Emphatic
125. metal	Metallic
126. poet	Poetic
127. ocean	Oceanic
128. prophet	Prophetic
129. athlete	Athletic
130. enthusiasm	Enthusiastic
131. energy	Energetic
132. angel	Angelic
133. science	Scientific
134. chaos	Chaotic
135. war	Warlike
136. life	Lifelike

137. busy	Businesslike
138. child	Childlike
139. dead	Deathlike
140. dog	Doglike
141. king	Kinglike
142, quarrel	Quarrelsome
143. tire	Tiresome
144. weary	Wearisome
145. trouble	Troublesome
146. fear	Fearsome
147. hand	Handy
148. frost	Frosty
149. heart	Hearty
150. earth	Earthy
151. bush	Bushy
152. business	Busy
153. dog	Doggy
154. fish	Fishy
155. juice	Juicy
156. laze	Lazy
157. noise	Noisy
158. room	Roomy
159. shade	Shady
160. speed	Speedy
161. stone	Stony
162. silk	Silky
163. month	Monthly
164. week	Weekly
165. day	Daily
166. year	Yearly
167. woman	Womanly
168 man	Manly
169. shape	Shapely
170. low	Lowly
171. love	Lovely
172. king	Kingly

173. hour	Hourly
174. home	Homely
175. dead	Deadly
176. body	Bodily
177. anger	Angry
178 hunger	Hungry
179. custom	Customary
180. winter	Wintry
181. imagine	Imaginary
182. satisfy	Satisfactory
183. prepare	Preparatory
184. introduce	Introductory
185. explain	Explanatory
186. contribute	Contributory
187. advise	Advisory
188. obey	Obedient
189. neglect	Negligent
190. patience	Patient
191. valour	Valiant
192. observe	Observant
193. importance	Important
194. flat	Flatwise
195. length	Lengthwise
196. health	Healthwise
197. side	Sideward
198. south	Southward
199. north	Northward
200. down	Downward
201. on	Onward
201. home	Homeward

Addendum K

Formation of Verbs from Other Words

WORD	VERB
1. courage	Encourage
2. sure	Ensure
3. large	Enlarge
4. capsule	Encapsulate
5. circle	Encircle
6. rich	Enrich
7. snare	Ensnare
8. rage	Enrage
9. rapture	Enrapture
10. noble	Ennoble
11. grave	Engrave
12. light	Enlighten
13. list	Enlist
14. live	Enliven
15. kindle	Enkindle
16. joy	Enjoy
17. join	Enjoin
18. graft	Engraft
19. franchise	Enfranchise
20. feeble	Enfeeble
21. danger	Endanger
22. counter	Encounter
23. compass	Encompass
24. code	Encode
25. close	Enclose
26. cash	Encash
27. case	Encase
28. force	Enforce

29. able	Enable
30. slave	Enslave
31. gulf	Engulf
32. trust	Entrust
33. fold	Enfold
34. power	Empower
35. body	Embody
36. brace	Embrace
37. broil	Embroil
38. bold	Embolden
39. bitter	Embitter
40. battle	Embattle
41. balm	Embalm
42. light	Enlighten
43. moist	Moisten
44. mad	Madden
45. hard	Harden
46. glad	Gladden
47. flat	Flatten
48. bright	Brighten
49. black	Blacken
50. tight	Tighten
51. short	Shorten
52. sharp	Sharpen
53. sad	Sadden
54. stiff	Stiffen
55. just	Justify
56. beauty	Beautify
57. electricity	Electrify
58. notice	Notify
59. simple	Simplify
60. false	Falsify
61. fruit	Fructify
62. pure	Purify
63. dear	Clarify
64. solid	Solidify

65. glory	Glorify
66. stupid	Stupefy
67. person	Personify
68. liquid	Liquefy
69. peace	Pacify
70. certain	Certify
71. terror	Terrify
72. fertile	Fertilize
73. solemn	Solemnize
74. equal	Equalize
75. drama	Dramatize
76. sympathy	Sympathize
77. empathy	Empathize
78. memory	Memorize
79. people	Popularize
80. nation	Nationalize
81. modern	Modernize
82. peril	Imperil
83. poor	Impoverish
84. pose	Impose
85. pound	Impound
86. print	Imprint
87. prison	Imprison
88. press	Impress
89. pregnant	Impregnate
90. plant	Implant
91. person	Impersonate
92. part	Impart
93. pale	Impale
94. mobile	Immobilize
95. migrate	Immigrate
96. humble	Humiliate
97. vigour	Invigorate
98. liberty	Liberate
99. captive	Captivate
100. differ	Differentiate

101.	substance	Substantiate
102.	clean	Cleanse
103.	cloth	Clothe
104.	breath	Breathe
105.	bath	Bathe
106.	fond	Fondle
107.	spark	Sparkle
108.	hand	Handle
109.	calm	Becalm
110.	little	Belittle
111.	siege	Besiege
112.	friend	Befriend
113.	guile	Beguile
114.	dazzle	Bedazzle
115.	deck	Bedeck
116.	moan	Bemoan
117.	numb	Benumb
118.	grudge	Begrudge
119.	strife	Strive
120.	belief	Believe
121.	half	Halve
122.	gift	Give
123.	shelf	Shelve
124.	company	Accompany
125.	bush	Ambush
126.	base	Abase
127.	credit	Accredit
128.	mass	Amass
129.	sure	Assure
130.	sort	Assort.
131.	flower	Flourish
132.	distinct	Distinguish
133.	fine	Refine

Index

A

Adjective Phrases	92
Adjectives, kinds of	62, 63, 73, 74
adverbial clauses	49
Adverbs	102
Adverbs of time	11, 38, 43, 58, 77
adverbs phrases	115
Articles	22

B

Building of words	128, 160

C

comparison of adjectives	86
Creative Writing	169
Curriculum Vitae	171

F

Formation of adjectives	89
Forming of adverbs	100
Functional Writing	170
Future Continuous	83
Future Perfect	69

G

Gerund — 108

H

Homonyms — 162

Homophones — 160

I

Infinitive — 147

Informative Writing — 170

N

Nouns — 30, 31, 32

P

Paraphrasing — 166

Participles — 148

Past Continuous — 48

Past Perfect — 70

Phrasal Nouns — 109, 117

Position of adjectives in sentence — 85

Possessives Case — 71, 72

Prepositions — 65, 94, 99

Present Continuous — 38, 39, 40

Present Perfect — 58, 59, 69

Pronouns — 61, 62, 63, 64, 65, 66

Punctuation — 73, 82, 90

Punctuation Activities — 82, 90, 96, 105, 111, 119, 125, 133, 139, 156, 170

R

Reading Activities   15, 26, 36, 54, 67, 72, 79, 92

97, 105, 108, 111, 119, 125, 133, 139, 144

151, 156, 164

S

Sentences   20, 27, 28, 42

Simple Past   43, 44, 46, 48

Speech, Direct and Indirect/Reported   114

Spelling rules   26, 57, 175

Summarising   167

T

Tenses, Simple Future   77

Tenses, Simple present   11, 12, 17, 23

V

Vocabulary Activities   13, 16, 19, 24, 41, 51, 71

81, 95, 103, 110, 118, 123, 132, 137

143, 149, 154

Voice, Active and Passive   31, 137